Transfiguration

Rob Marshall is a parish priest, writer and broadcaster. He has presented BBC Radio 4's *Thought for the Day* for more than two decades. He is an Honorary Canon of the Cathedral and Abbey Church of St Alban and Rector of Digswell, Welwyn Garden City. Before returning to parish life, he spent much of his ministry in communications.

He is a frequent pilgrim visitor to the Church of the Transfiguration on Mount Tabor in Galilee and more locally to the pilgrim sites of Iona and the north of England where he was born.

Transfiguration

Rob Marshall

CANTERBURY
PRESS
Norwich

© Rob Marshall 2023

Published in 2023 by Canterbury Press
Editorial office
3rd Floor, Invicta House,
108–114 Golden Lane,
London EC1Y 0TG, UK

www.canterburypress.co.uk

Canterbury Press is an imprint of Hymns Ancient & Modern Ltd
(a registered charity)

Hymns Ancient & Modern® is a registered trademark of
Hymns Ancient & Modern Ltd
13A Hellesdon Park Road, Norwich,
Norfolk NR6 5DR, UK

British Library Cataloguing in Publication data

A catalogue record for this book is available
from the British Library

978-1-78622-531-3

Typeset by Regent Typesetting
Printed and bound in Great Britain by
CPI Group (UK) Ltd

Contents

The Second Week of Lent – Being a Disciple

The Third Week of Lent – Tabernacles

The Fourth Week of Lent – Clouds

The Fifth Week of Lent – Glory

Holy Week – Transfiguration of Suffering

Eastertide – God's *Yes* to Who Jesus Is

For Jackson

Introduction

You are warmly invited to follow in the footsteps of Jesus on this Lenten pilgrimage. We follow our Lord and his three closest disciples up to the top of a high and lonely mountain where he will be transfigured. There we will spend some time pondering the scene, taking in the view of our lives today and reflecting.

We will journey from low down in the Jezreel Valley in Galilee to the summit of Mount Tabor – the probable venue of Jesus' Transfiguration. Then after some time on the mountain, we will descend again to the plain and to the inevitability of what Jerusalem holds for our Lord.

Each of the 50 pilgrim steps marks a day of Lent culminating with the Eastertide season. Peter, James and John are totally unaware of how events in Jerusalem will unfold before Jesus' death and resurrection. They are equally unprepared for an unexpected glimpse of the glory of God in the presence of Moses and Elijah.

Much ignored until relatively recent times, the Transfiguration poses a unique challenge for the days between Ash Wednesday and Eastertide. Throughout the 50 short pilgrim reflections covering the whole of Lent, we will consider afresh the implications of God's glory for the world, the Church and ourselves.

There is a short reflective question after each of the 50 pilgrim steps and some questions for readers or small groups at the end of each week.

Acknowledgements

Thank you to all pilgrims who have made the physical journey with me to the Mount of the Transfiguration.

For those who have been unable to make the journey in person, I hope these reflections will enable you to see why this theme is more than relevant for Christians today.

Thank you to those friends and colleagues who have provided fresh quotes about what the Transfiguration means to them.

Thank you too to the Revd Selina Evans for proofreading and valuable suggestions, and to Christine at Canterbury Press for her extraordinary patience.

It's challenging enough writing one BBC *Thought for the Day* script: writing 50 has been an exciting challenge!

Rob Marshall
Digswell
Pentecost 2023

The Bible Accounts

Mark 9.2–8

After six days Jesus took Peter, James and John with him and led them up a high mountain, where they were all alone. There he was transfigured before them. His clothes became dazzling white, whiter than anyone in the world could bleach them. And there appeared before them Elijah and Moses, who were talking with Jesus.

Peter said to Jesus, 'Rabbi, it is good for us to be here. Let us put up three shelters – one for you, one for Moses and one for Elijah.' (He did not know what to say, they were so frightened.)

Then a cloud appeared and covered them, and a voice came from the cloud: 'This is my Son, whom I love. Listen to him!'

Suddenly, when they looked around, they no longer saw anyone with them except Jesus.

Matthew 17.1–8

After six days Jesus took with him Peter, James and John the brother of James, and led them up a high mountain by themselves. There he was transfigured before them. His face shone like the sun, and his clothes became as white as the light. Just then there appeared before them Moses and Elijah, talking with Jesus.

Peter said to Jesus, 'Lord, it is good for us to be here. If you wish, I will put up three shelters – one for you, one for Moses and one for Elijah.'

While he was still speaking, a bright cloud covered them, and a voice from the cloud said, 'This is my Son, whom I love; with him I am well pleased. Listen to him!'

When the disciples heard this, they fell face down to the ground, terrified. But Jesus came and touched them. 'Get up,' he said. 'Don't be afraid.' When they looked up, they saw no one except Jesus.

Luke 9.28–36

About eight days after Jesus said this, he took Peter, John and James with him and went up into a mountain to pray. As he was praying, the appearance of his face changed, and his clothes became as bright as a flash of lightning. Two men, Moses and Elijah, appeared in glorious splendour, talking with Jesus. They talked about his departure, which he was about to bring to fulfilment in Jerusalem. Peter and his companions were very sleepy, but when they became fully awake, they saw his glory and the two men standing with him. As the men were leaving Jesus, Peter said to him, 'Master, it is good for us to be here. Let us put up three shelters – one for you, one for Moses and one for Elijah.' (He did not really know what he was saying.)

While he was speaking, a cloud appeared and covered them, and they were afraid as they entered the cloud. A voice came from the cloud, saying, 'This is my Son, whom I have chosen; listen to him.' When the voice had spoken, they found that Jesus was alone. The disciples kept this to themselves and did not tell anyone at that time what they had seen.

2 Peter 1.16–18

For we did not follow cleverly devised stories when we told you about the coming of our Lord Jesus Christ in power, but we were eye-witnesses of his majesty. He received honour and glory from God the Father when the voice came to him from the Majestic Glory, saying, 'This is my Son, whom I love; with him I am well pleased.' We ourselves heard this voice that came from heaven when we were with him on the sacred mountain.

The Week Before Lent – Preparation

'The Transfiguration is really puzzling – not quite fitting with the flow of the gospel narratives and not easy to understand. And yet it draws me in.'

(Professor David Wilkinson, St John's College, Durham)

Ash Wednesday: Introduction

It Draws Us In

The Transfiguration is the Gospel reading in the Church of England's lectionary for the Sunday before Lent. This is no mere coincidence. The lectionary planners plainly knew what they were doing. So, as we too explore this fascinating episode in the life of Jesus, it is best that we better acquaint ourselves with the New Testament evidence. There are three Gospel accounts. John omits it. And there is a reference to it in 2 Peter. These are printed in previous pages for your reflection and study.

Indeed, I suggest a real familiarization with the detail of the three Gospel accounts. Though essentially the same, each story has its own style and emphasis. Perhaps jot down some of the 'exclusive' features of each interpretation of what happened on the mountain and what strikes you most about them? How is Luke's story different from that of Mark? Matthew's account varies in several ways. There is much to explore in the different accounts of the same story. And it is in the differences of emphasis that some of the most important spiritual truths of the story emerge.

Looking at the 2 Peter account will also help. As an eye-witness account of the apostles (for that is clearly what it is) this reference may well be the earliest account we have. Is this how the Gospel writers themselves heard of what happened on the mountain directly from the mouth of the apostle Peter? Try to bear this account in mind throughout. We will also see that it has special resonance once Easter arrives and we look to the greater future glory still to be revealed once for all.

A better understanding and knowledge of the biblical evidence is obviously an advantage as we make this Lenten pilgrimage. We will, of course, look more closely at why St John chose not to include the story in the Fourth Gospel, both as Easter approaches and at Easter itself. I agree with the comment by Professor David Wilkinson at the beginning of this section that 'the Transfiguration is really puzzling and not easy to understand. Yet it draws us in.'

Certainly, it draws me in because it is rich with symbolism and mystery.

To summarize the main events: about a week after what are probably the events at Caesarea Philippi (which we will explore further on Day 3), Jesus takes Peter, James and John to the top of a high and lonely mountain. There he is transfigured. Moses and Elijah appear alongside him. There is also a cloud. A voice issues a divine command from within the cloud. Peter has a starring role and talks of tabernacles. After the whole scene has ended, an important conversation takes place between Jesus and his friends. Then it is almost as if nothing had happened on the mountain top. The disciples say nothing about it. Why do you think this is? How could they possibly not talk about such a huge moment and keep the whole thing a secret?

Today's Thought: As you reflect on the three accounts, is there an image or moment that resonates with you?

Thursday: Journeying

Life-changing Journey

Most people like travelling. It is what humans have done since earliest times – going from one place to another for a variety of reasons. Modern transportation systems now offer even more options. We can generally move around much more freely than ever before, though I know some local bus services are hugely frustrating.

Commuting habits have changed even more since the 2020 pandemic. People now spend more time in their own neighbourhoods and less time in city centres. While engaging with colleagues in the workplace is obviously valuable, the virtues of homeworking, along with the flexibility and convenience it provides, are some of the positive changes that have happened. As major conurbations reimagine their futures, the drop in commuting brought benefits to the environment and local economies.

Journeys feature prominently in the books of the Bible. Think of all those dramatic journeys with the great patriarchs and prophets, including Abraham, Moses and Elijah in the Hebrew scriptures. There, while many local communities stay the same for generations, the main characters often seemed to be called by God to move themselves and sometimes others on huge life-changing journeys.

Jesus rarely stays still in the Gospels. He journeys constantly from one part of the Holy Land to another. He is rarely in the same place for more than a few days. His final journey to Jerusalem has huge significance – it is the ultimate journey of sacrifice and love. Pilgrims have made the same journey on pilgrimage to Jerusalem in the footsteps of Jesus ever since, to reflect on that sacrificial love.

A pilgrimage is a unique journey with much more about it. Pilgrimage demands serious preparation. It usually involves the company of others, often strangers. As well as practical travel, usually to a place of spiritual significance, there is also a spiritual dimension involving prayer, the reading of scripture, the celebration of the sacraments and perhaps the renewal of vows. Pilgrimages are often as challenging as they are enjoyable. They are nearly always life-changing in some way. The BBC recently featured several pilgrim journeys with 'celebrity' strangers coming together to visit the likes of Santiago de Compostela and Iona. Most recently, seven well-known pilgrims of different faiths and none travelled along the northern route of the Fatima Way in Portugal. It was another extraordinary journey of discovery, new friendships and learning from each other.

When I think of journeying and pilgrimage, I automatically think of Iona. Columba left Ireland for an unknown destination and God led him to this remote Hebridean Isle where Christianity took root in Britain for the first time. Most of us have a favourite place where we can reconnect with God to resurrect our spirits. Iona is mine. Similarly, for Jesus and his disciples, the Transfiguration journey will be like no other as they journey to their destination where glory and light will unexpectedly abound. It almost certainly would have remained as a key moment in their minds for ever.

Today's Thought: Think of a favourite journey or destination of yours. What makes it so special?

3

Friday: Who Is This?

An Astonishing Realization

The question *who is Jesus?* dominates not only the Transfiguration story but the build-up to the story and their descent from the summit of the mountain. It is after an event which happened a few days before the Transfiguration took place that the party of four made the climb and we will presume that the Gospels are referring to what happened at Caesarea Philippi (modern-day *Banias*).

The story of what took place at Caesarea Philippi is a classic episode in all three Synoptic Gospels. It is the ultimate feedback session. The Gospels tell us that Jesus and all twelve disciples 'went on to the villages around Caesarea Philippi" (Mark 8.27ff.), during which Jesus asks his disciples a basic question: 'Who do people say I am?' The disciples give a variety of replies based largely on hearsay – what others are saying. The late Pope Benedict XVI in his book *Jesus of Nazareth* writes, 'At certain key moments, the disciples came to the astonishing realization: This is God himself. They were unable to put all this together into a perfect response.' Aware of the disciples' confusion, Jesus then asks them the same question directly. Peter speaks up, 'You are the Messiah' (v. 29), and, not for the first time, Jesus intriguingly commands them to tell no one – a secret we will return to later.

It seems clear that Jesus asks the question about his identity because he really wanted to know what the message on the street was and what his disciples thought. He is not asking how he's doing but who they think he is. His question is about identity and disclosure. Who has clicked yet?

It seems, then, that it is for a reason that all three Synoptic Gospel writers place the story of the Transfiguration immediately after Caesarea Philippi. They see the two as connected. Confession leads to manifestation. What follows on the mountain is a visual demonstration of Jesus' messiahship, visualizing Peter's confession of faith a few days before.

Judaism, as a religion in the Holy Land, was in a state of flux during the time of Jesus. This was an occupied land, and the Jewish people were very much up against it. It is from this context that the Messiah appeared in the most unexpected of ways. There were many differences of opinion between the various Jewish sects in and around Jerusalem as to when and how the Messiah would come. But, overall, Jewish expectation was still rooted in a basic belief that, after many false dawns, the Messiah would once for all finally redeem his people. The question Jesus is asking is, have people's eyes been opened yet? Surely it is no coincidence that the visual demonstration of God's glory on the mountain follows soon after.

Jesus was probably relieved that Peter had 'clicked' before the Transfiguration unfolds. There is, no doubt, a poignancy to the climb up the mountain: a combination of recognition, revelation and understanding.

Today's Thought: Have you experienced a moment of absolute clarity, a moment of profound understanding of an aspect of faith?

4

Saturday: Days

Where Can We Live But Days?

We thank you that you have brought us safely to the beginning of this day. This is how the Church of England Morning Prayer service begins each day. It certainly helps separate one day from the next even if they do arrive more and more quickly the older we get. Another day has dawned. Let us make the most of it.

In the Transfiguration story, Mark and Matthew indicate six days between what we suggest is Caesarea Philippi and the arrival on the mountain. So, about a week. But in the Bible, 'days' are regarded as theologically significant – they are gifts from God to make the most of. From the accounts of the creation in the book of Genesis to the number of days between the crucifixion and resurrection, to the number of days in this Lent season – all have significance of various kinds.

In the creation stories, God frames each working day between evening and morning. The work done constitutes a day. Each is declared as 'good'. Morning and evening follow each other rhythmically to make up another day full of creative work, until the Sabbath day on which God rests (Genesis 2.3). The Sabbath is declared holy from the start. Days instil a pattern for living through creation.

The Hebrew word for 'day' – *yom* – means 'as opposed to night'. It can, however, mean the whole 24-hour cycle embracing both evening and morning. But by the time of Jesus and with the people of occupied Jerusalem asking many questions about God's future intentions, the notion of 'day' develops clear futuristic (known as eschatological) overtones: 'But the day of the Lord will come like a thief. The heavens will disappear with a roar ... and the earth and everything done in it will be laid bare' (2 Peter 3.10). Yes, this Day of the Lord is partly to be feared if one's own house is not in order. We return to this significant theme at Eastertide.

The poet Philip Larkin, who worked in the library of my hometown of Kingston Upon Hull, wrote a glorious poem called 'Days'. He asks simply and cleverly, 'what are days for?' before acknowledging, 'where can we live but days?' The reference to the passing of days before the Transfiguration heightens my awareness, when I read all three accounts, that time is always moving on and God's purpose is framed more and more each day that passes.

These days in Lent are celebrated in the hymn for the season, 'Forty days and forty nights'. It is an encouragement to seize the initiative of preparing for the astonishment of the resurrection glory soon to be revealed. Later in the hymn we sing, 'Keep, O keep us, Saviour dear, Ever constant by your side, That with you we may appear At th'eternal Eastertide.' Every day is a pilgrim day with Jesus. In the wilderness. On the mountain. Underneath the cross. At the empty tomb. We live in these days. Making the most of each of them is a daily challenge.

Today's Thought: Pray perhaps with a bit more reflection than usual these familiar words – 'Give us this day our daily bread.'

A Prayer

Almighty Father,
whose Son was revealed in majesty,
before he suffered death upon the cross:
give us grace to perceive his glory,
that we may be strengthened to suffer with him
and be changed into his likeness, from glory to glory;
who is alive and reigns with you,
in the unity of the Holy Spirit,
one God, now and for ever.
Amen

(Collect for the Sunday next before Lent, Common Worship)

Questions

Having read the three Gospel stories of the Transfiguration, look particularly at St Luke's version and ask – why
does this perhaps stand out the most?

Have you ever been on a pilgrimage? If you have, what
things about it do you still remember? If you haven't, what
would most attract you to the idea and where would you
most like to go?

David Wilkinson describes the Transfiguration story as a
puzzle. What bit of the story puzzles you most?

The First Week of Lent –
The Mountain

'The Transfiguration is an unveiling – a tantalizing glimpse into what we cannot yet fully grasp but will one day see fully.'

(The Revd Nicola Vidamour, writer and Methodist minister)

5

Sunday: Mountain

Apart, By Themselves

Mountains play a significant role in many religions, including Judaism and Christianity. They are usually the venues for great acts of revelation. The Transfiguration is just one example. The writer of 2 Peter describes it as 'the sacred mountain' and the Gospel stories that it was 'apart' from other local mountain ranges.

Any contemporary pilgrim to the Holy Land cannot help but notice the multiple small mountain ranges visible from any coach or car window. One cluster of mountains after another represent the stories of God and his people through the critical stages of salvation history. For such a small country, the mountainous scenery is truly remarkable and varied. I never cease to be impressed with how local guides so easily and clearly know when one mountain range ends and another begins. One reason is that each usually has some significance for our understanding of the Bible.

It's worth mentioning a few of the most famous biblical mountains here. Mount Zion is one of the most well known, but how small it is when you first see it from the centre of modern-day Jerusalem. It was on a rare snowy January day in Jerusalem that I first set eyes on Mount Zion, a small, unassuming hill on the bend of a twisting road, yet it is the place where God dwells (Isaiah 8.18; Psalm 74.2), where both the Lord is King (Isaiah 24.23) and David is proclaimed king (Psalm 2.6). It is astonishing to see it.

Mount Moriah is most closely associated with Abraham and the sacrifice of his son Isaac. It is also where Solomon built the Jerusalem Temple. Moses and Mount Sinai are synonymous with the giving of the law and the making of the new covenant. Mount Horeb is where Elijah encounters God, along with Mount Carmel where he battled against Baal. The presence of Elijah and Moses on the Transfiguration mountain is no real surprise: the disciples did not seem fazed. Mountains had always been part of the story. There is a real sense of fulfilment here on the Transfiguration mountain.

But which mountain is this one? I suggest we simply accept Mount Tabor as the place (Mount Hermon has been another candidate), not least because it is where the current pilgrim churches of the Transfiguration are located and it is visited daily by hundreds of contemporary pilgrims. Viewed from the roads below, Tabor is, as the Gospel accounts attest, high and apart – geographically isolated. In the region, it certainly sticks out a mile. In Mark's original Greek text, we are told that Jesus 'brings up' Peter, James and John to a mountain, *oros*, which is both high, *hypsèlon*, and apart, *kat*.

We arrive full of expectation at the summit. There are already many questions emerging for the disciples. Why here? Why have they been chosen? What about those who have been left behind? If a mountain is usually a place of revelation in the Bible, what is about to happen here and why? The beginning of the first Sunday of Lent sees us elevated, with a better view of our lives, full of expectation as we arrive at the summit.

Today's Thought: What is your favourite place with a view, and why?

6

Monday: Solitude

The Joy of Retreat

The fact that the Transfiguration group are apart and alone on the top of the mountain suggests that Jesus really did intend them to have some time away from the rest and from the crowds – some solitude in order to be witnesses of whatever was about to be revealed.

In Paris, I once bought a second-hand copy of *Les Caractères* by the French moralist and philosopher Jean de la Bruyère. It made a big impression on me. All unhappiness, he writes, comes from our inability to be alone. He believes that the great misfortune of life is 'to be incapable of solitude'. But solitude does not always need to be something we experience alone: we may also seek it with a partner or friends or a small group of people. We certainly need to differentiate it from loneliness, which we will discuss later. Solitude can be wonderfully creative, giving the space and time that is so often lacking in modern-day living.

I have certainly found that I now enjoy increasing amounts of time alone. Just getting away, even for a short time, is both challenging and rewarding. Not being afraid of the silence when all our gadgets and devices are turned off is quite a feat. Of course, we need to be sensitive to others who might share our lives. We don't want to cut them off or make them feel uncomfortable. But positive isolation and withdrawal from the din of life can be surprisingly rewarding.

Being solitary need not exclude doing things. Indeed, people are often more productive if they have time and space to think.

Being quiet and able to focus better on tasks in hand can be hugely creative.

So, the small Transfiguration group is elevated, isolated and detached. Luke alone adds that the reason for their ascent up the mountain was to have some prayer time together. Jesus has organized an impromptu retreat. This is a common theme elsewhere in Luke: 'But Jesus often withdrew to lonely places and prayed' (5.16). Luke's use of the word 'lonely' here can be misleading. In his book *Reaching Out*, the Dutch Catholic theologian Henri Nouwen, for instance, observes that 'the movement from loneliness to solitude ... is not a movement of a growing withdrawal from, but rather a movement towards, a deeper engagement in the burning issues of our time'.

Luke even suggests they all needed a nap (28.32). We will look at how important tiredness and sleep is to our spiritual lives later. As far as the disciples are concerned, however, their withdrawal from the others remains a mystery to them, at least for the moment.

The isolation of the Transfiguration party is critical to our story. God is going to be able to address the special assembly directly on the mountain top. What a gathering it is. The Spanish mystic, Teresa of Avila, stresses that place is all important: 'We have no wings to go in search of him but have only to find a place where we can be alone – and look upon him present within us.'

Today's Thought: How would you describe the difference between solitude and loneliness?

7

Tuesday: Prayer

Hope in God

One of the things we often do during the period of solitude offered by Lent is to focus on our prayer life. And we know that Luke's story of the Transfiguration has a much greater emphasis on the importance of prayer than Mark's and Matthew's versions. Luke is clear the reason Jesus brought Peter, James and John up to the summit of the mountain was in order to pray and that, *as he was praying*, the appearance of his face changes. Indeed, of the nine prayers of Jesus recorded in the Gospel of Luke, seven are only found here. He even includes two parables about prayer – the friend at midnight (11.5) and the unjust judge (18.1).

On any pilgrimage, prayer is central to the whole journey and experience. It is part of the preparation, the setting out, the journey itself and the return. Through the offering of intercessions and the asking for God's blessing, the daily pilgrimage activities, whether with others or alone, at home or elsewhere, is a journey of discovering the inner self. On pilgrimage, pilgrims often experience the draining away of stress: a gradual refocusing on the power of God in all things takes over. Of course, it's not an easy process.

Individual pilgrims approach prayer differently. I have witnessed that personally on pilgrimages I have led. Reflecting on scripture seems to be more popular than ever, alongside Christian meditation and mindfulness. Candles and icons can be a great help, others walk or sketch or sing. The *how* does not really matter. It is the act of prayer itself that counts.

The Bedfordshire parish of Elstow asked me to lead them on a pilgrimage to Columba's island of Iona. After a great week of prayer and worship together, the group presented me with a beautiful copy of John Bunyan's quintessential pilgrim manual, the *Pilgrim's Progress*. Bunyan was baptized at Elstow Abbey – now their parish church of Elstow – and is a local hero. Dipping into the book again recently, I was reminded of how Bunyan talks simply about an engaged kind of prayer that is both connected and meaningful: 'When thou prayest, rather let thy heart be without words than thy words without heart.' We are not just to go through the motions when we pray. Bunyan urges us to immerse ourselves in prayer of all forms and to live the pilgrim experience of encounter with God.

The book of Psalms is a wonderful example of prayers lived out in the rough and tumble of life. They no doubt played a huge part in Jesus' own spiritual journey as the prayer book of the synagogue in which he was handed the scroll to read in his hometown of Nazareth. Psalm 43, for example, describes how, after experiencing rejection, the faithful are brought to the holy mountain – the very place where God dwells (v. 3). Here God is praised through prayer with a confident conclusion, and the message is clear: 'Put your hope in God, for I will yet praise him, my Saviour and my God' (v. 5).

Today's Thought: The how and when of our prayer life can be very different throughout the journey of life and faith. What has been helpful to you?

8

Wednesday: Sadness

The Globalization of Emotion

When the Scottish musician Lewis Capaldi watched a candid TV documentary about his life, with which he had cooperated, he said: 'It's a sad watch. I didn't expect my life to be so sad.' There is no doubt when watching the film, and particularly his struggles with Tourette's syndrome, that he is rightfully proud of his ability to be honest in this *warts-and-all* depiction of his own life's struggle. The trappings of celebrity status may offer temporal luxuries, but no amount of fame or money can compensate for a prevailing sense of sadness.

The journalist Tom Whipple observed in *The Times* that, more and more, and for a whole variety of reasons, people are emotionally distressed: 'They are sad in Suriname. They are worried in Westphalia. They are angry in Algeria. And we aren't doing too well in Britain either.' It seems that increasing numbers of people are suffering from being sad. There are clear issues around poor mental health. There are not the resources to deal with the number of individuals who admit that they need help.

A starting point, it would seem, is simply to talk more openly about the subject as Capaldi did. Sadness (which is not the same as loneliness, which we will reflect on later) needs to be outed. Very often, as a parish priest, when someone says to me, 'I feel so sad,' they don't always realize that even wanting to talk about it is already a positive step in the right direction. It is far too easy to bottle up our feelings and to avoid talking, thus deepening an inner sense of sadness and despair.

Note that all three Transfiguration stories say that Jesus is seen to be talking with Moses and Elijah. What they were talking about (it would have been quite something to be in on that conversation) is not clear. But talking with and to God is certainly a central feature of the Hebrew scriptures, represented here by Elijah and Moses.

To have faith and to believe in God is to communicate openly with him. If we have anxieties, concerns or worries, we are encouraged to bring our troubles to the Lord. To talk about them and to listen. This takes us all the way back to finding time to say our prayers regularly whatever our mood. Bringing to God all our joys and reasons for sadness and asking him to hear us as we also listen to whatever he is saying to us, can bring about real transformative change to our mood and our lives.

Prayer is just one way in which light can infuse our mood and pierce darkness. The vision on the mountain is certainly full of light and hope. Finding a way to see what God is trying to show us here is what our exploration of the Transfiguration is all about this Lent.

Today's Thought: 'It is better to keep silence and to be, than to talk and not to be' (St Ignatius of Loyola).

9

Thursday: Sleep

The Impact of Sleep Deprivation

A tabloid newspaper recently claimed that Britain is becoming 'a nation of zombies, with half of us getting too little sleep every night'. Apparently, 91% of us regularly wake up in the middle of the night. Dr Guy Meadows, a sleep specialist, believes that sleep is one of our most important things – for both physical and mental health – and it's clear that sleep deprivation is having a big impact on people's lives.

The high percentage of people struggling to rest and to sleep is serious. From my experience, in parish life, people talk about this often and it is a cause of great concern that they are unable to sleep properly. It can be the second most popular topic of conversation after the weather. Lent, as a time of retreat and recovery, might well be an excellent time to try to address any underlying causes of sleep deprivation and to find new ways to relax.

I grew up listening to *Thought for the Day* and to the great Rabbi Lionel Blue. I never imagined that one day I would sit in his seat in the BBC's *Today* studio. He had a knack of being conversational and humorous. His talks used to jump from one topic to another, often eliciting a smile from the listener (what's he going on about now?) until, brilliantly, with a final flourish he would make his point, deliver his 'thought'. Once he began by admitting that worry was sometimes the cause of sleep deprivation, before going on to explain how he tackled it: 'If I can't sleep from worry, I think up some Jewish light bulb jokes which help; it's better than counting sheep.'

Only Luke has the detail that Peter and his companions 'were very sleepy' on the mountain before 'they became fully awake' just in time to see the glory of God. This could be symbolic of their lack of awareness as to what was going on but there is no doubt that physical tiredness probably played a part, for this is not the only time sleep features prominently in Luke. Much later, on the night of Jesus' arrest in the Garden of Gethsemane, Jesus goes to pray, then comes back, only to find the disciples 'asleep, exhausted from sorrow' (22.45), before asking, 'Why are you sleeping? ... Get up and pray so that you will not fall into temptation' (v. 46).

The psalms again seem to confirm that sleep is equated with relaxation and peace. The opposite is also true. For the psalmist, there is no explanation for self-imposed sleep deprivation: 'I will allow no sleep to my eyes or slumber to my eyelids' (Psalm 132.4), and a desire for real sleep is yearned for. Rabbi Lionel is not alone in acknowledging that a good night's sleep is surely a good starting point for what lies ahead during the rest of the day as it unfolds.

Today's Thought: 'In peace I will lie down and sleep, for you alone, LORD, make me dwell in safety' (Psalm 4.8).

Friday: Place

We Love This Place, O God

Before the end of this first week of Lent, we consider the pilgrim place of the Transfiguration. This will be an easy exercise for those who have been able to visit Mount Tabor in the Holy Land. You can close your eyes and go back there and imagine the place over again. If you have not visited this pilgrim place, perhaps let me try to paint a picture.

Mount Tabor is an isolated hill in the Galilee region. Any Holy Land map will easily locate it. It is 11 miles from the sea of Galilee, at the eastern end of the Jezreel valley. It is visible for miles around.

The delightful Arab villages of Daburiyya, Shibli and Umm al-Ghanam are at the foot of the mountain. The faces of these villagers are well known to regular pilgrims: they are hardworking, quiet, family orientated – they have worked near Mount Tabor for generations. Some make their living from the Transfiguration pilgrimage site as drivers, shop owners and guides.

A coach can only go so far. There is a large parking area at the base of the mountain. From there, locals drive pilgrims around a series of 39 hairpin bends. Queues for the transfer cars are common.

There are two Christian monasteries on the summit. I have not been able to visit the Greek Orthodox community as it is generally closed to tourists, but I have stayed for a few days on the Franciscan site on the south-east side and shared fellowship with the monks there. The Catholic Church of the Transfiguration is splendid. The hymn 'We love this place, O God' is always in my heart as I approach its simple steps and climb even higher, as if to the summit of the mountain itself.

There has been a place of worship on the site since the Crusader period. The present church, however, was designed by the architect Antonio Barluzzi and completed in 1924. Inside there is a resplendent main altar with mosaics depicting the Transfiguration, and two chapels at the rear celebrating the lives of Moses and Elijah. Over the years, I have had the privilege of celebrating Mass at all three altars as well as some of the outside pilgrim spaces also reserved for groups to worship.

The choice of venue for any pilgrimage is important. Each pilgrim place or destination resonates and speaks to those who visit. Pilgrimage venues are sometimes called 'thin places' because the gap between heaven and earth is hardly noticeable. Mount Tabor is our thin pilgrimage place this Lent. It is a real living place with its own unique history and character. We join with others, marvel at the sight, observe the view, smell the smells and drink in the atmosphere. The gloriousness of this mountain, place of pilgrimage, means different things to different people. But it is certainly a place of glorious solitude, deep prayer and with the imminent promise of the true light piercing the darkness of the world.

Today's Thought: Have you visited a thin place, where heaven meets earth and God is present?

Saturday: Context

Taking In The View

Perhaps we can now understand a little better why the Transfiguration story is the lectionary Gospel passage for the Sunday before Lent. Having prepared for the ascent with Jesus and his friends and having arrived at the summit, we realize that something dramatic is about to happen. Not only are we to see who Jesus is after all that happened at Caesarea Philippi, but we are to realize the demands of discipleship on those who see what happens, and consequently on us also.

We drink in the view and imagine and admire the place. Using our imagination we imagine how Peter, James and John must have felt. They had been told not to say anything to anyone after Peter had confessed that Jesus is the Messiah at Caesarea. They had left behind the other nine disciples. They arrive on the mountain top tired but ready to pray. This is their context. They soon gain a sense of perspective and see the bigger picture. For me the Transfiguration is a gradual realization of the sheer enormity of God's plan.

Examining the context in which we live often reveals how quickly life moves on. Circumstances do not stand still. Relationships change. We become older and, hopefully, wiser. Every day, there are new issues and challenges. It is a 'coming together' moment in the gospel story as a variety of factors join together to provide a unique set of challenges as we face the future as Jesus' disciples.

Next week we explore what it means to be a disciple of Jesus today, in our time and place. We are invited each day to consider what being a disciple really means in the light of everything that is soon to be revealed on the holy mountain.

The question facing each pilgrim is – can I really rise to the challenge and respond to Jesus' call, just as the disciples did? Am I prepared, ready even, to face the true cost of discipleship? Like Peter, James and John, we see now the complex and competing factors combining to show how the pilgrim path of discipleship is never easy.

The Church Fathers wrote about this as early as the first century and Christian writers and theologians have reflected on it ever since. For example, Thomas Aquinas wrote in the thirteenth century that, 'although our view of the most sublime things is limited and weak, it is a great pleasure to be able to catch even a glimpse of them'. Much earlier, in the fifth century, St Augustine of Hippo suggested that faith is to believe what you do not yet see because the rewards for such faith are that our eyes will ultimately be opened to the one true light.

But this demands that we continuously see our lives as part of the bigger picture. We need to get a view of our lives and absorb what we are truly facing. It is hard to do that from day to day. The mountain helps here. Nicola Vidamour at the start of this chapter said, 'The Transfiguration is an unveiling – a tantalizing glimpse into what we cannot yet fully grasp but will one day see fully.'

Today's Thought: Are you able to catch a glimpse of the glory of God?

A Prayer

Almighty God,
by the prayer and discipline of Lent
may we enter into the mystery of Christ's sufferings,
and by following in his Way
come to share in his glory;
through Jesus Christ our Lord.
Amen.

(*Alternative Collect for Lent 2*, Common Worship)

Questions

Climbing a mountain is physically hard work – it takes determination and sometimes courage (think of all those hairpin bends on Mount Tabor). Is this an important aspect for you of the Transfiguration story on our journey?

How comfortable are you with being in your own company?

Do you find that sleep patterns have changed or are changing? How does sleep fit in with faith?

The Second Week of Lent –
Being a Disciple

'On reading the account of the Transfiguration I am always heartened and strengthened in faith and hope – rather like the disciples themselves who witnessed the glorified Lord. It also puts me in mind of the hymn sung at my confirmation some seventy years ago now – "O Jesus thou hast promised, To all who follow thee, That where thou art in glory, There shall thy servant be." A great encouragement to keep at it!'

(Bishop David Hope, a former Archbishop of York)

12

Sunday: Discipleship

God's Grace in Action

Writing in his classic work *The Cost of Discipleship*, the twen-tieth-century Christian martyr Dietrich Bonhoeffer believes grace is the key ingredient in the working out of what it means to be a disciple of Jesus: 'It is only because Jesus became like us that we can become like him.' Jesus offers us unqualified love, and we must then respond accordingly. Grace is essential in the personal call of Jesus. We respond to the offer of God's grace and we follow him as appropriately as we are able.

As contemporary disciples of Jesus we surely need to hold on to Bonhoeffer's brave challenge of accepting the unqualified love of God in our hearts. These cannot be just words. We experience this love through God's grace.

The Transfiguration story is a key stage on the road to God's grace being revealed. The disciples' love of Jesus is increasing but Jesus' friends are not always that quick off the mark in understanding the enormity of what true discipleship involves.

After Caesarea Philippi, the Transfiguration is certainly a visual aid for the disciples to better understand God's grace in action through Jesus. The glory is glimpsed. But first there is more work to do: the rejection, arrest, suffering and death of Jesus, followed by a period of enormous uncertainty. On top this, for the moment, everything must remain a secret, nothing must be talked about or revealed outside of the group.

In that well-known story, which is part of the big narrative of Holy Week and not that long after Peter had witnessed the Transfiguration, he falls at a first hurdle. In the courtyard, Peter has a perfect opportunity to show his love of Jesus. When challenged to say he is a disciple he says the opposite (*I do not know him*) for fear of his life (Matthew 26.69–75). With all the best intentions in the world, if the pressure mounts and the going gets tough, what are we do to in the face of our human frailty and weakness?

In seeking God's grace to do our best, we set ourselves a Lenten challenge to be better disciples. We will never get it entirely right and our human weaknesses will occasionally get in the way. But just as Bonhoeffer clearly saw beyond the weakness of humanity and looked to the promised glory of the Father so can we. The glory may not yet be tangible or complete, but the promise is real, and a demand of faith is made of each of our Lord's disciples. The daily challenge is to believe and to trust; not to waiver by holding fast to God's grace.

Today's Thought: '*O Holy Spirit, Give me faith that will protect me from despair, from passions, and from vice; Give me such love for God and men as will blot out all hatred and bitterness; Give me the hope that will deliver me from fear and faint-heartedness. Amen*' (Dietrich Bonhoeffer, Letters and Papers from Prison).

13

Monday: Witnesses

The Need for Wisdom

One of the first questions new disciples often ask is 'Why me?' People try to explain how it feels to be called by God but are often bemused. Why did God call me to faith at this moment? Yes, what's the job description? It is a conversation that ordinands, those who feel chosen by God to be ministers in the Church, often have with their priest and bishop. It has taken God all this time to call me and suddenly the calling came.

Some have called the three chosen disciples in the Transfiguration story Jesus' friends. I always wonder whether of the 12 disciples these were Jesus' closest friends and allies. The question why Peter, James and John, rather than the others, were chosen has preoccupied some commentators. What about the other nine who were left behind? How did they feel? How would you have felt being left behind to twiddle your thumbs? The author of 2 Peter suggests they are 'eyewitnesses', as if to confirm that all that took place did indeed take place.

The same three disciples also appear separately from the others at various times, namely, at the healing of Jairus' daughter (Luke 8.49–56) and in the Garden of Gethsemane, which we have just mentioned (Matthew 26.36–38). It is generally assumed that, among the disciples, these three were Jesus' most trusted inner circle. We all have friends or work colleagues that we are closer to than others.

We cannot be sure how the other disciples responded to being left out of some of the more significant events in Jesus' life. What we do know is that each had a role to play. Human psychology suggests that, as often happens today, leaders seem to have certain people whom they turn to at moments of challenge or calamity in search of sound and honest advice – perhaps it is the same with you?

Being called is one thing. Being called to witness to a wider group is another, bringing with it added responsibility. In today's culture, if we witness something either good or bad, people often hesitate before deciding to put themselves forward as a witness because there are often untold consequences.

Over a period, the disciples understood this. Each in their own way. But in the world and Church today, being a disciple of Jesus still makes demands on us at witnesses. We are not always well received. The context is increasingly challenging, certainly in Britain, to be a public witness for Jesus. We might consider the following before moving on.

First, we are *chosen* by God, and we have a choice as to how to respond. Second, we are *privileged* to be called even though we may have legitimate questions as to why we, rather than another, have been chosen. Third, from the moment of our being called we have *new responsibilities*. Returning to our original question – 'Why me?' – it might have to be enough to say that the answer lies ultimately in God's wisdom. That is not a cop-out: we might just never fully understand it.

As our lives go on from day to day and year to year we continue to witness God's love in new ways. We can only pray more deeply for wisdom to respond appropriately as Jesus' disciples today.

Today's Thought: How would you define the wisdom of God that we are called to pray for?

14

Tuesday: Fear

The Fear of the Lord is the Beginning of Wisdom

On the mountain, Peter, James and John were terrified. Whichever of the Bible accounts you read, this is hardly surprising. From our earliest years, when we are fearful of all sorts of things, we continue to be affected, sometimes inexplicably, by a variety of things throughout our adult lives. But the disciples experienced a fear upgrade. Many New Testament translators of the original Greek regarding this particular aspect of the Transfiguration story suggest 'terror' rather than 'fear', but either way the disciples were not at all sure what was going on. Apparently, they were terrified.

There are different takes on the fear aspect in the Transfiguration story. In Mark the reference to the disciples being frightened is personified in the person of Peter who, it is claimed, did not know what to say because they were frightened. In Luke, they are reported to have 'entered the cloud' at the same time as being afraid of the scene before them. But in Matthew's account the fear is exacerbated when they hear the divine voice and 'they fell face down to the ground, terrified'. Jesus responds by urging them not to be afraid.

The most famous verse in the Bible about fear is to be found in Proverbs 1.7: *The fear of the LORD is the beginning of knowledge, but fools despise wisdom and instruction.* The Hebrew word used here – *yirah* – can mean awe, respect, reverence, worship, as well as fear. The suggestion clearly is that in the presence of God there is nothing to fear if we have faith enough to be disciples and, therefore, also witnesses of the divine glory.

It is with this backdrop to his own spiritual journey that Jesus enters the wilderness on his own for 40 days and 40 nights. As a young Jewish man in first-century Palestine, he experienced fear, terror and multiple temptations. Each Lent is a fresh opportunity to confront our own fears in the same way that Jesus did. Some of our fears are rational. Others plainly are not. It might be a good idea to jot down the things we used to fear but which no longer bother us. Or we could consider what we are now most fearful about and for, terrified even, as we face the future. This might lead to a time of meditation or prayer, bringing our hopes and fears out into the open, in the light of our pilgrim journey this Lent to the top of this extraordinary mountain.

On the summit, God provides Jesus' friends with the perfect antidote to all their fears. The glory of God alone, it would seem, casts out all fear, changes everything if we have faith to accept what is offered to us. There is nothing more to worry about when the promise of future glory is complete. The hymn 'Just as I am without one plea' (Charlotte Elliott) offers reassurance and hope that, by staying close to God, we can openly offer our fears to him, remembering the message of the angels both to Mary in Nazareth and to the shepherds in the Bethlehem fields: 'Do not be afraid.' We note that they recognized the divine intervention, responded to it in faith and openly believed in the glory that was revealed.

Today's Thought: A verse from Elliott's hymn, 'Just as I am'.

Just as I am, though tossed about;
With many a conflict, many a doubt.
Fightings within and fears without;
O Lamb of God, I come.

Listen to this hymn, or read it again, and as you do, bring to God any fears you may have noted down.

15

Wednesday: Speechless

Shut Up, Peter! God is Here

The UK weekly Sunday *Observer* newspaper once produced a cartoon called 'Speechless'. It depicted a series of isolated small creatures of different shapes. They were each trying to communicate with one another but failing to do so. Communication was simply not happening. The drawing depicts for me life as it is for many people today. The speech balloons said and asked: 'It's too quiet in here now', 'I think I can hear you?', 'Will I ever see you again?' But no one was listening.

On the mountain it is Peter, often the centre of attention, who is rendered speechless. We are told that he was so flabbergasted by what was taking place that he did not know what to say. Or, as we have already concluded, it might be that fear got the better of him. In Luke's version he does say something without realizing what he was saying. How many times have you asked yourself the question, 'What am I going on about?' Or been in any kind of meeting with others when one person is just talking for the sake of it?

The conundrum is always choosing when to stay quiet and when to speak out. Deciding not to say anything for fear of exacerbating a situation at home, work or among friends is usually a proactive conscious decision. The result is often positive. By not stating your position you can become a focus of unity for others and be regarded instead as a good listener. It is also true when replying to emails: particularly those we may find annoying. Pause before replying; think about it and then reply.

A lot of the time, however, we are like Peter. We either do not know what to say or we say something inane – ridiculous even – and later regret it. I have often wondered if Peter really did regret saying what he said. Maybe it was just part of the unfolding drama. He is uncertain, fearful even. He says the first thing that comes into his head. It is a connection between fear and awe, which combine to result in the disciples' self-appointed spokesman being lost for words. Only then does God intervene and command him (and the others) to be quiet.

It was a former Archbishop of Canterbury, Michael Ramsey, who told me while I was studying in Durham, 'God says to Peter, shut up Peter, God is here. Be quiet Peter, God is here. Enough words. Enough words.' Being a disciple carries with it clear responsibilities around sensitivities in communicating the truth about Jesus. It is rarely easy. Sometimes it is best to remain quiet. At other times words are given to us and we should speak out. Knowing which is the best option remains a daily challenge for any disciple.

Today's Thought: Help us to speak when it's the right time to speak. And to be quiet when saying nothing is the much better option.

16

Thursday: Good to Be Here

Wish You Were Here?

Whatever our view as to whether Peter should have kept quiet or spoken out, it is what he said that interests us today. First, he declares how good it was to be there. Then he suggests building three tabernacles – one each for Elijah. Moses and Jesus.

I am not good with silence when in the company of another person. Indeed, I am usually the first to break it, which, I realize, can be very annoying. I am talking here about silence for the sake of it rather than a silence that is planned. There is also the danger of then asking a simple question, such as 'How are you?', which another person might find more difficult to answer than we expect. It might be the last question someone wants to answer if they are having a bad day or if life is particularly challenging. More often than not, for an easy life, they will reply that all is good, even if it is not.

We have suggested that being a disciple involves God's grace accompanying us on every step of the pilgrim way. Such grace is most valued and welcome when we least feel like playing the role of a disciple. It is not always easy to be upbeat and positive. Usually, we just do our best. Peter, without realizing it, declares that, despite all the questions, contradictions and uncertainties that being a disciple of Jesus carries with it, it is indeed good to be here.

During this pilgrim journey, we will occasionally consider the importance of some of the titles associated with the life and ministry of Jesus, and ask what their meaning is in context and what they say to us today. Noticeably, each of the Gospels has Peter addressing Jesus differently – *rhabbi* (Teacher) in Mark, *kyrie* (Lord) in Matthew and *epistata* (Master) in Luke. It might be worth considering what each of these special titles says about this significant moment between Peter and Jesus. Which do you prefer? Peter just needs to talk. 'It is good to be here,' he declares.

Perhaps, in the face of so much uncertainty in the world today, Peter's mantra, 'It is good to be here,' is not such a bad one for us each day. Whatever the news headlines or what the day might personally have in store for us. It is good to be here. Whatever fears we might be harbouring. It is good to be here. We do not know what tomorrow will bring. For the moment, however, it really is good to be here.

There is a hymn that utilizes Peter's expression – 'T'is good, Lord, to be here' – and it is still one of the best-known traditional hymns associated with this story. It is Peter's hymn. It reveals a real positivity and happiness at being with our transfigured Lord. Of course, our fears can be overcome. We will listen from now on to what the Lord is saying to us. We will consider better whether to speak or to remain silent. Remembering and reflecting on the glorious vision on the mountain, and the sense of sheer joy of being present with Jesus, is a way of embracing a sense of our love and hope as disciples of Jesus.

Today's Thought: 'It is good to be here.' Do we truly believe it? We should not forget this moment as we reflect on the glory of God in Jesus.

17

Friday: Resilience

He Knows You Can Do This

Most days the news agenda is full of examples of fortitude and resilience. With so much bad world news to digest it is good to see stories of people showing real fortitude by overcoming various hurdles to reach their goal or even to help someone else.

The most obvious examples are those who deal with a serious or terminal illness and speak publicly about it in order to raise awareness of it in others. The journalist and broadcaster Bill Turnbull presented the national BBC breakfast television programme for many years. Once diagnosed with prostate cancer he urged men of an appropriate age to be tested and to deal with any problems as early as possible. The campaign continued until Bill died a few years later. Many others have similarly raised awareness and saved many lives.

Think also of the women and men living with various disabilities who compete in international sport and break records across a range of sports and physical activities. How do they have the courage to pick themselves up and really go for it? Their resilience is an example to all. It is astonishing.

On the mountain top, after the glory has been revealed, Matthew relates that Jesus came over to the disciples and touched them. He told them to 'get up' and not to be afraid. Those of you who have read the New Testament in any detail know that this is something Jesus often does. He urges people literally to 'get up', to prove to them and to those watching that some miraculous happening has taken place, thus showing that God is alongside them if they have faith.

When, for instance, Jesus enters the house of Jairus' daughter who, according to messengers, had already died (Mark 5.21–end), he takes her by the hand and says to her, '*Talitha koum*' ('Little girl, get up'). The 12-year-old is brought back to life. Those witnessing it are 'completely astonished'. There are many other examples too, such as when Jesus says to a man who was lame, 'Get up! Pick up your mat and walk' (John 5.8).

In our parish, one of the most poignant services we hold regularly is a monthly healing service during which we offer anointing for the sick and suffering. Obviously, the invitation is open to all. People usually come, however, because they, or someone they know or love, is facing a particular challenge. Very often, the healing they are seeking is for a physical ailment. However, increasingly, the ministry of healing is sought for a range of related mental health conditions. Extreme care and serious pastoral oversight is necessary here. The prayer is always the same: that the healing touch of Jesus will make them whole.

When Jesus urges his disciples on the transfiguration mountain to 'get up', he acknowledges their human frailty while at the same time embodying God's ability to change or transform anything that is weighing us down and testing our resilience.

Today's Thought: Matthew tells us that Jesus reached out to the disciples, encouraging them with words. In what way are we able to walk alongside others as they attempt to 'get up'.

18

Saturday: Call to Action

We Need to be Kinder to Ourselves

> Before He had the world's foundations laid
> God's love was in his only Son displayed,
> And that same love extends to all mankind,
> Oh, what amazing grace when eyes once blind,
> Behold his perfect glory.

This is the final stanza of Dorothy Bull's poem 'Prospects of Glory' which explains how, when a person finally beholds God's glory, their eyes are opened and the love of God is shared.

We started this week reflecting on discipleship in the context of the Transfiguration. Bonhoeffer expressed the importance of love and grace in action. I would hope that, as we end the week, we are more convinced than ever that being a disciple of Jesus today is, above all, a call to make a real difference to the people and situations we meet.

With so much challenging news to deal with every day, as well as what we are also wrestling with in our own lives, life can be disorientating. This is particularly and increasingly so for many young people I meet in my ministry and as chaplain to several schools. The past years have not been kind to them and there is a great deal of supportive pastoral work to do.

But it is not all bad news. The older I become the more I appreciate the inherent kindness and goodness of most of the often-unseen people I meet in my work. Or simply going about my daily life. They are everywhere. Whether teachers, national health service staff, people trying to help others in a variety of practical ways – it is not all doom and gloom when it comes to human kindness and generosity. Some of my favourite social media videos are about pure acts of kindness: there are thousands upon thousands of examples of human positivity.

Melanie Philips wrote in *The Times*: 'Beneath the disorientating roar of our era's cultural and political cannon fire we see countless acts [of kindness] around us all the time. Telling ourselves that humanity is inherently cruel is a distortion. We need to be kinder to ourselves than that.' Being kind is not dependent on any person's religion or faith. There are many who would say that they are not believers, but they are still kind. But being a disciple of Jesus inevitably carries with it an inherent responsibility to share love and kindness with others.

Bishop David Hope, the former Archbishop of York, believes the Transfiguration story focuses on our fortitude and resilience in keeping our promises to Jesus. It is about keeping at it, persevering in all things. As he says at the opening of this section, the Transfiguration 'puts me in mind of the hymn sung at my confirmation some seventy years ago now – "O Jesus thou hast promised, To all who follow thee, That where thou art in glory, There shall thy servant be." A great encouragement to keep at it!'

Today's Thought: How are we going to be able to keep at it through thick and thin?

A Prayer

Be a smooth path below me,
a kindly shepherd behind me
today, tonight, and forever.
Alone with none but you, my God,
I journey on my way;
what need I fear when you are near,
O Lord of night and day?
More secure am I within your hand
than if a multitude did round me stand.
Amen.

(St Columba of Iona)

Questions

To what extent do you feel equipped to be a disciple of Jesus today? What are you comfortable with and what things would you like to be better at as a witness for Jesus?

Peter says, 'It's good to be here.' Is that a mantra you share with him when you wake up every morning? If not, how can this story on the mountain help reassure you?

Groups of friends are important and it's fascinating how we choose either to spend a lot of time on our own or in a smaller group where we feel safe and supported. What kind of a friend are you?

The Third Week of Lent – Tabernacles

'The Transfiguration reminds me of sitting watching an early morning sunrise over Iona. As it rises, it becomes more blinding. I think of the four elements of life, Earth, Air, Fire, and Water. This reminds me of Jesus who created all this and in whom we live and move and have our being.'

(Sister Jean RSCJ)

19

Sunday: Tents

Jesus Is There

In this third week of Lent our attention turns to the question of the tents or tabernacles – perhaps the most unusual aspect of our story. The suggestion of building tabernacles is all part of Peter not knowing what he was saying. Simply put, he offers to build three tabernacles, one each for Moses, Elijah and Jesus.

The reference to tabernacles is a strong link between the Old and New Testaments – the new fulfilling the old in and through the person of Jesus. In the Hebrew scriptures a tabernacle is a 'place of dwelling'. Whenever the people of Israel were on the move, the tabernacle was erected as they set up camp. It was a de facto temporary sanctuary and place of worship. Instructions were clearly laid out as to how it should be constructed (Exodus 25.8, 21–22). The people knew that God could be found here. The people would enter the tent. It became a temporary centrepiece of essentially nomadic worship. There was a firm belief that God provided the faithful with a safe place: 'In you, LORD, have I taken refuge' (Psalm 71.1).

God is now about to play a central role in the mountain scene, and the tabernacle heralds that moment. Like many momentous events that are meaningful and indescribable, we do not want the moment to come to an end. God is here. Jesus is here. The Old and New Testaments are hereby joined together. We want to know that God will not leave the scene of revelation again. That he will stay.

Today, in many churches, a tabernacle is where Jesus is to be found. It is a place set aside for the reservation of the holy Eucharist for distribution to the sick and dying. On many occasions I have received a call, at various times of the day or night, requesting the sacrament be taken to someone who is in the latter stages of life. Visiting the tabernacle while on the way to a person who is sick, one finds there in this most holy of places – often lit by a simple candle denoting God's healing spirit – Jesus present in his body and blood. The sense of God ever-present remains as strong today. It is a remarkable part of the journey through life.

Peter certainly wanted to prolong the scene. He did not want Moses, Elijah or Jesus to depart from them. His hope is that God will stay there for ever.

St Thérèse of Lisieux, whose basilica is in the heart of the lovely Normandy town that has adopted her, underlines the personal aspect of divine realization represented by the tabernacle: 'Do you not realise that Jesus is there in the tabernacle expressly for you – for you are not alone? He burns with desire to come into your heart.' The tabernacle is central here. Jesus is in our midst. God is with us through his Spirit.

Today's Thought: Imagine any holy place you love and work out why it is special to you. Do you return to it often in your mind's eye?

20

Monday: Hebrew Scriptures

A Conundrum

In general, it is fair to say that Christians do not read the Old Testament as much as they might. Speaking once with three bishops at the same time – all of whom visit a different church just about every weekend – they said that it was noticeable how many churches did not include an Old Testament reading at all. In recent times, to avoid using the word 'old' to describe something that is not old at all to Jewish worshippers, the term 'Hebrew scriptures' is sometimes used instead. However, the world 'old' is obviously in stark contrast to the essentially 'new' covenant which Jesus seeks to establish.

The Transfiguration has a key role to play in terms of the coming together of the two Testaments. The story's motifs are intertwined and only fully fathomable from the point of view of both sections of the Bible. In many respects, the Transfiguration is a story of transference – a vivid portrayal of Jesus assuming the joint mantles of Moses and Elijah as one era is transfigured before the disciples into a new and fulfilled age. God authenticates the moment with an unusual, divine personal intervention which we reflect on later.

I recently undertook a period of sabbatical study looking afresh at the Dead Sea Scrolls. This was done in memory of Dr Philip Davies, my teacher, friend and a devoted scholar of Qumran (where the Dead Sea Scrolls were found). I spent the early part of 2022 in Manchester updating myself on current scholarship around the findings at the Dead Sea. Not only did this reignite my interest in Old Testament history, it also changed my understanding of the state of Judaism in the time of Jesus. The context here of Old Testament fulfilment and what the Jewish scholars, chief priests and scribes were expecting is crucial.

Our Lord inaugurates a new covenant. He gives us a new commandment. Jesus talks openly of a new exodus. This is the nub of the kingdom of God (see the parable in Luke 5.33–39) which is at the heart of the 'new' testament as a fulfilment of all that has gone before. Of course, as Christians, we must revere and hold fast to the books of what we have traditionally called the Old Testament. We cannot understand either the Transfiguration or the Gospels without it.

The biblical scholar Professor John Barton has recently written two books in which the centrality of many Hebrew texts is underlined and explained. In his *A History of the Bible* he writes, 'The relation of Old Testament to New is thus at the heart of Christian theology, but it is a conundrum rather than a clear doctrine, a paradox.' This is very much the case for us on our pilgrimage. In every respect the central motifs of the Transfiguration story – tabernacles, Moses, Elijah, cloud, voice and mountain – are both a conundrum and a paradox. They bring the old and the new together in the eternal presence of Jesus. We thank God today for the unique library of Hebrew texts and ask for the discipline to read and understand them more.

Today's Thought: A challenge! Think of a favourite story from the Old Testament – try to identify some of the key motifs in that story that make it stand out for you.

21

Tuesday: The Courage of Elijah

His Courage Outlived Him

There are stories of examples of amazing courage every day. People wake up without knowing what they might be called upon to do later that day. Unexpectedly, people respond without hesitation to help others, often showing real bravery in the process. To save a life, assist someone who is injured, rescue a stranded animal, enter a situation of great danger – there are countless good news stories like this in any one week. There are some annual awards called the Pride of Britain, in which stories of remarkable courage are told about people reacting selflessly, without a thought for themselves.

Elijah has many human attributes in the Bible, but courage is chief among them. Today's Thought (below) encourages us to read Elijah's life as told in 1 Kings 17—19. It should only take a few minutes and it is a great story, introducing you again to a key figure in the Transfiguration account, who represents vulnerability, honesty and courage.

Elijah's courage is rooted in a surprisingly uncomplicated faith. He says it as it is. He believed there was only one God and vehemently fought idolatry. He lived a life of service. He did whatever God told him to do. He was alert to life's dangers and zealous in his work. At times, he just wanted to give up, and tried to do so several times, but God would not allow it. Because of his courageous legacy, Elijah is still venerated today by Jews, Christians and Muslims for his faithfulness.

Elijah's appearance with Moses on the Transfiguration mountain has traditionally been regarded in purely ambassadorial terms. The two figures were there to represent the prophets and the law. But in both cases, much more can be written about their lives.

Elijah's courage outlived him. The faithful, waiting effectively for the coming of the Messiah, believed they would see Elijah again. Malachi 4.5 highlights how, during the times of the prophets, Elijah was synonymous with better times to come: 'See I will send the prophet Elijah to you before that great and dreadful day of the LORD comes.' That is surely why Peter, James and John are not surprised to see Elijah on the mountain with Jesus (though how they knew it was him is a serious question). Neither is it unusual for the bystanders near the cross of Jesus in Jerusalem hearing him cry out to God at the point of death (see Mark 15.35) to suggest, 'Listen, he's calling Elijah', when he was in fact calling his Father. They still associated Elijah with the coming of the Messiah and had heard how John the Baptist had been confused with Elijah, suggesting the latter had come back to life. Elijah was clearly current in the expectation of the faithful in the time of Jesus concerning a Messiah's arrival.

The strong Old Testament overtones surrounding the Transfiguration are rooted in the work of Elijah and Moses. In Elijah's case, news of his courage, bravery, faith and persistence in doing God's work come as no surprise to those on the mountain. Elijah is a crucial wheel in the cog as God's glory is now finally to be revealed, once and for all.

Today's Thought: Take some time to read 1 Kings 17—19 to explore the wonderful work of Elijah the prophet.

22

Wednesday: Moses and a New Exodus

The Passion Brings Salvation

Succession planning is a relatively modern concept in business, education and other walks of life. It's not always as obvious in the life of the Church, however. I'm a trustee of several charities where succession planning is often discussed. We are guided to think of how decisions made today will affect tomorrow and be built on in the future. At a crucial moment on the top of the Transfiguration mountain, only Luke explains that Moses and Elijah are talking about Jesus' *exodus* which he is to *accomplish* in Jerusalem. The verb *accomplish* is just as important as the noun *exodus*.

Moses is the central figure in the Old Testament. He has been described as the founder of monotheistic belief and his life is told across many of the Hebrew scriptures. He is chiefly known as the lawgiver and the leader of his people from captivity to freedom. Moses is given the Ten Commandments by God on Mount Sinai and delivers the Israelites held captive in Egypt by leading them through the waters of the Red Sea. Moses initiates a covenant between God and his people.

So it is against this background and with this understanding in mind that Moses is seen handing over the covenant and exodus themes to Jesus the Messiah in a radically new context. As we established on Day 5, the mountain links both Testaments together as a venue. The disciples' minds must have been scrambled at this point. What is Jesus' role to be in all of this? In her book *Transfiguration*, Dorothy Lee explains, 'What is to be fulfilled is God's plan for salvation, manifested in the death, resurrection and ascension of Jesus along with the sending of the Spirit on the gathered church in Jerusalem, the city of destiny.' Jesus had said several times to his disciples that he was to suffer and to die before rising again. What is not clear in his conversations on the mountain was whether those listening equated Jesus' work with what had happened during the lifetime of Moses. Later – when St Paul started writing his letters as the early Church grew – the link was established, cemented and celebrated.

That is surely why Moses is the most cited Old Testament figure in the New Testament. Paul, immersed as he was in Jewish expectation, realizes how Jesus now takes up the whole work of Moses so that our Lord can be described as the *new* Moses, inaugurating a *new* covenant through the giving of a *new* commandment. One of the most important New Testament verses is Matthew 5.17. Jesus explains that he has not come to *abolish* the old order but to *fulfil* it. That fulfilment now takes place on the mountain before our eyes. The prophet Elijah and Moses together see Jesus' radiant glory. They surely know that the longed-for moment of redemption is not far away.

As mentioned before, at the entrance to the Church of the Transfiguration on Mount Tabor, there are two glorious chapels dedicated to Moses and Elijah. Both figures longed to see this day. These chapels are reminders that by being present with Jesus on the mountain, Moses and Elijah remind us that this was part of God's plan all along. As Pope Benedict in his *Jesus of Nazareth* expounds, 'This Passion brings salvation: that it is filled with the glory of God; that the Passion is transformed into light, into freedom and joy.' The baton has been passed on. A new exodus now takes place before their very eyes.

Today's Thought: How has your understanding of the Exodus story changed, if at all, after reading Luke's story of the Transfiguration?

23

Thursday: Refugees

Their Death Changes the World

Refugees are rarely out of the news. They have dominated decades of headlines. I am writing this as, not for the first time, thousands of displaced people have been forced to flee their homeland in Sudan because of a civil war. The stories I read are hugely personal and devastating. Families torn apart. Children separated from parents and grandparents. It has been the same story with Ukraine following the Russian invasion. Closer to home, refugees trying to reach the United Kingdom are forever the source of debate and discussion.

If the tent or tabernacle is regarded as a place of sanctity and worship, where God is to be found wherever the people landed, it is important to take a moment during this Lenten pilgrimage to pray for and remember all displaced peoples. For those who have not experienced it, it must be a truly shocking and obviously life-changing ordeal. For the rest of the international community, how to deal with thousands of displaced people with nowhere to call home is the source of huge diplomatic and political inertia. Christians often say that we must do something to help these people. The question is where or how can we provide a sanctuary – a tabernacle – for them among us? The tabernacle is a symbol of hope where God is to be found, even for those without a place to call home, for God is alongside them.

When our parish book club read Christy Lefteri's novel, *The Beekeeper of Aleppo*, many perceptions of refugees held by members of the group were profoundly changed and challenged. We read of a woman blinded by grief travelling from Syria to the United Kingdom, accompanied by her devoted husband Nuri, who used to keep bees in Syria. For these good-mannered, kind and trusting souls, the battle between darkness and light went on and on continuously: 'Sometimes we create such powerful illusions, so that we do not get lost in the darkness,' says Nuri, before adding, 'Where there are bees there are flowers, and wherever there are flowers there is new life and hope.'

On our pilgrim journey, we surely hold in our prayers before God those who have nowhere to call home and for whom their current journey has no destination. If the tabernacle motif means anything for a displaced person, it represents a refuge and sanctuary, which we as members of the international community must find a way of providing. When 27 occupants of a dinghy carrying people from France across the Channel died after it capsized in the darkness, the Bishop of Leeds, Nick Baines, said on *Thought for the Day*:

> I don't know the names or circumstances of those who have died, but their death changes the world. Every person matters, absolutely – not just those we deem acceptable. Naive sentiment? Maybe, but it also happens to go to the heart of what Christian faith refuses to negotiate.

Today's Thought: I remember reading a few years ago of how a sheet of blue plastic became home for refugees who had crossed thunderous waters. This flimsy sheet was a place of safety – it was their temporary home.

24

Friday: Memory

Forgetting How to Remember

Peter's reference to tabernacles invokes memories of Israel's past and allows Jesus to demonstrate how what we have learned from history not only frames our futures but allows us to understand them. But are we losing the ability to remember? I sometimes wonder how modern technology, which affects more and more aspects of our lives, will leave its mark. Artificial intelligence (AI) is just another development bringing both revelatory progress and allegedly huge threats to our way of life as we understand it. In the early days of its development, AI researchers signed an open letter from the Future of Life Institute calling for a six-month pause on research so that policy could catch up.

It is uncertain what the effects on the human memory will be. After both my parents had died, I joined my brother and three sisters in sorting out the family home. We discovered a host of hard-copy tangible memories – photographs, certificates, notes, letters and school reports – few of which today's generation will be able to find in the future. It seems that we are collectively losing our ability to save things and remember things, because, with the advent of technology, we simply do not have to any more. Remembering things is no longer what it was. Memory, archiving and saving has changed for ever because of the internet and digital revolution, which have transformed the notion of memory itself.

As human beings and Christin pilgrims on a journey together, we grapple daily with the increasing challenge of remembering things. Much Christian understanding and liturgy is rooted in the act of remembering. Scripture, words, promises and instructions enable us to interpret and live the pilgrim life. A great deal of Christian worship is rooted in remembering and repeating. We 'call to mind' things and do things 'in remembrance'.

In terms of memory, the Transfiguration is a visual demonstration of the interaction of the past, the present and the future. On the mountain, the disciples call to mind all that has happened in the past and look to a new future in the light of the transfigured Jesus. The past frames the future and we understand ourselves more as a result. We call to mind the past to reassure us in the present as we look faithfully to the future. But things are changing more and more quickly around us.

Alongside the relentless innovations of technology, we should try not to lose the art of remembering. Calling to mind the past enables us to better understand the challenges facing us into the future as our pilgrimage continues.

Today's Thought: Telling stories is how we remember and pass on those memories. Will you tell the stories of your own pilgrimage of faith?

25

Saturday: Icon

His Mercy to Us

The Orthodox tradition, which places greater significance on the feast of the Transfiguration than is so in the West, also has a higher view of the importance of icons. They are, in many ways, aids to teaching and spiritual reflection. They are similar to a homily or sermon, teaching something of the mystery of Christ and of his words and works, and a great help for those societies where people are unable to read and write.

If you can, look up online an image of the icon believed to have been painted by Theophanes the Greek around 1403. It is housed in the Tretyakov Gallery in Moscow. While battling leukaemia, and in the latter years of his life, Bishop Kenneth Stevenson acknowledged the personal importance of this particular icon to his spiritual journey. In his final book *Rooted in Detachment, Living the Transfiguration*, he explains how this icon is a gateway to the saving events of the gospel.

The colours used in the icon are particularly magnificent, reflecting Jesus' glory. The contrast is stark between the whiteness of Jesus' Transfiguration and the earthly ground. The disciples look completely taken aback, shocked and in awe of the sight they are presented with. The rays of white, depicting the glory of God, reach the disciples via straight, white lines which link up with them. This is a theme to which we will return later in our journey.

It is, however, in the portrayal of the tabernacles along with Moses and Elijah that the icon is particularly magnificent. Moses is holding a book (probably the Torah) and Elijah projects out his hand like a modern-day TV presenter introducing Jesus to those around him, with the tabernacle-type tents under their feet. As we come to the end of a week mulling over the tabernacle in the Transfiguration story, this icon is a splendid way of remembering the merging of the old with the new and the transformation of the future.

Sister Jean RSCJ, who ran the House of Prayer on Iona for many years, used to sit in the beautiful retreat house sitting room in the morning and evening to read and reflect. For her, along with the retreat house chapel, the place was a sanctuary, like a tabernacle, where Jesus could always be found. The view from the window, of Iona, is of a genuinely thin place. Gazing through the window is like looking at an icon. The gap between earth and heaven is almost non-existent. The glory is tangible. As Sister Jean wrote at the start of this section, 'This reminds me of Jesus who created all this and in whom we live and move and have our being.'

Whatever picture you frame in your own mind as to what the Transfiguration looked like – cherish and ponder it. The icon may be a help. Gaze on the view – a place where your mind and heart can return often to take in the vista and simply drink it all in.

Today's Thought: 'And we all, who with unveiled faces contemplate the Lord's glory, are being transformed into his image with ever-increasing glory, which comes from the Lord, who is the Spirit' (St Paul, 2 Corinthians 3.18).

A Prayer

Glory be to you, O God,
For the gift of life
Unfolding through those who have gone before me.
Glory be to you, O God,
For your life planted within my soul
And in every soul coming into the world.
Glory be to you, O God,
For the grace of new beginnings
Placed before me in every moment and encounter of life.
Glory, glory, glory
For the grace of new beginnings in every moment of life.
Amen

(*J. Philip Newell,* Celtic Benediction: Morning and
Night Prayer*)*

Questions

The plight of refugees is never out of the news. How do you
reconcile your Christian faith with the perilous journeys of
those without anywhere to call home?

If you ever visit a cathedral or a church where the sacrament is lit in a tabernacle, what is your response to this
great symbol of Christ being always with us?

Memory is being shattered by the onset of technology. Our
young people keep very little physical records of great
life events. How will museums reflect our times to future
generations? Mary Beard once said they will be full of
different types of trainers!

The Fourth Week of Lent – Clouds

'The Transfiguration of Jesus reveals the glory which God has in mind for every human being. As Paul said, we are being transformed into his image, from glory to glory.'

(Bishop Richard Harries, a former Bishop of Oxford)

Sunday: Cloud

They Were Afraid as They Entered the Cloud

The fourth week of Lent is a time to focus on the single cloud that invades the sky above the mountain as Jesus is transfigured. Not everyone has been in an aircraft. But it is wonderful to witness clouds close up for the first time. I can still remember the first time I saw them above the London skies. With a few bumps we ascended through some thinly scattered, wispy clouds, only to do the same when descending safely again to land.

The transfiguration cloud raises three major questions:

- Why does God choose to intervene directly here?
- How do we respond to the drama of what then happens?
- When we consider the suffering going on in the world, what is God saying in the light of all that lies ahead through Passiontide, Holy Week and on through Easter?

Most of the time it is rare to see any clouds on Mount Tabor. Experiencing an isolated cloud is even rarer. Imagine how the disciples might have felt. Mark describes the cloud as appearing and covering them. It is not clear if it is Moses, Elijah and Jesus who are covered (more likely) or whether the three disciples were cloud-covered as well. In Luke, the cloud appears while Jesus is still speaking and it covers 'them'. Additionally, in Luke, 'they were afraid as they entered the cloud'. Matthew recalls a much simpler version – while Jesus is still speaking a bright cloud covers them. A voice then speaks from the cloud.

Once again there are strong links here with the Hebrew Bible, in which the cloud is usually portrayed as the vehicle of God's presence (Psalm 105.39; Ezekiel 1.28). As far as our story is concerned, Exodus 24.15 also has a particular resonance: 'When Moses went up on the mountain, the cloud covered it.' In many Old Testament examples, God is hidden by the cloud.

It is, however, usually God's method of transport – the vehicle by which he can suddenly appear on the scene. This is certainly the case on Mount Tabor. No one expected to see a cloud and yet it is not a total surprise. This cloud, thankfully and inevitably, turns our attention to the future.

We acknowledge how the cloud is both a vehicle for God's presence and a source of divine communication. There is more than a hint of excitement and expectation in the air. What does the future hold? For sure, there will be turbulence. But on this special pilgrimage we are expectant and waiting as God arrives on the scene. As Bishop Richard Harries explains in our introduction to this section, the cloud marks a moment of revelation through which, as St Paul underlines, 'we are being transformed into his image, from glory to glory'.

Today's Thought: When are you most aware of God's presence with you?

An Extra Thought: Mothering Sunday

Spreading a Message of Love

In 2023 I was on the rota to present *Thought for the Day* on Mothering Sunday weekend. I explained to those listening that it is a moveable feast because it is celebrated three weeks before Easter on the fourth Sunday of Lent. This pattern started in the Middle Ages when children, often in domestic service, were allowed home to join their families and to worship in their 'mother' church. It was also known as 'Refreshment Sunday', when the solemn fasting of Lent was interrupted by the sharing of simnel cakes. Families reunited and gathered around the table.

Mother's Day is a much later, secular invention and the two have confusingly merged, though here in the UK the Christian calendar still determines the date.

Those preaching or speaking in churches on Mothering Sunday on anything to do with mothers or family life now need to reflect on how society has changed. I noticed in a wider inclusive language guide that the charity Oxfam recently instructed staff to use the word *parents* when describing family roles, rather than mother and father. This reflects what most schools do today: talking of parents and carers, ensuring that as many children as possible feel included.

In giving out bunches of flowers in church on Mothering Sunday, I always think it is worth remembering those for whom such a day is more than difficult. The writer Lizzie Lowrie pointed this out in her blog when she wrote, 'Every year those grieving the loss of a mother, those living with the struggle of infertility, those who've lost children, those who are single and long to be married with a family, and those who are hurt by or never met their mother can feel isolated.'

So, in our own times, how can Mothering Sunday speak to everyone, including those who genuinely feel excluded? If the Christian gospel is about anything, it is about love. Whether speaking about family life or being a good neighbour, Jesus persists across the Gospels with the theme that no one any longer needs be on the outside looking in: rather, everyone is welcome into the family of God, the only condition being that we show our love of God by how we treat and, yes, love one another.

Society is changing. It is certainly being more honest. While Mothering Sunday has traditionally been a way of celebrating one kind of loving, it is perhaps now an opportunity for us to think about how we can welcome everyone, with open arms, celebrating acceptance. It is a moment to ask ourselves if there are new ways for us all to choose love in our day-to-day lives.

Today's Thought: On this Mothering Sunday maybe we can ask of ourselves, how do we express the love of God that is available to everyone, without exception?

27

Monday: Epiphany

Perceiving Him More Clearly

After studying the Transfiguration for many years, describing the event as an epiphany is relatively new for me. The American theologian John Paul Heil has suggested in his monograph *The Transfiguration of Jesus* that this is the best word to sum up the totality of what we are presented with on the mountain. The introduction of the cloud, followed by the voice and the divine command, are among the main features of the story which suggest all of the essential ingredients of what might be termed an epiphany.

Epiphany, in Greek, means showing forth, revelation or manifestation. It is also the name of the Christian season after Christmas beginning with the arrival of the three Gentile kings, bearing their symbolic gifts of gold, frankincense and myrrh. Epiphany is the time in the year to recall God revealing the Logos (the Word made flesh) to the world. It underlines how Jesus is revealed through signs and wonders including his baptism and the wedding at Cana of Galilee, which is described as the first sign in John's Gospel.

Heil argues that the Transfiguration has, in the past, wrongly been described both as a *vision* and a *theophany* when it has always just been an *epiphany*. The story certainly has elements of what Heil calls a *vision* ('the seeing of a privileged group of supernatural phenomena located mainly in the heavenly realm'). The same applies to his definition of a *theophany* ('a disposition of literary motifs which describe the coming of God recognised by terrifying circumstances accompanying it').

But Heil is very clear that the Transfiguration is quintessentially an *epiphany* – a truly 'penny-dropping' moment in the life of the disciples. What is more, because the divine voice, which speaks from the cloud, is so direct, commanding us to listen to Jesus without any room for questioning, what we have in the Transfiguration is in fact a *mandatory epiphany*. God's command on the mountain top, in the Greek original, is an imperative. We have no choice but to listen. So, the whole party, gazing on this glorious sight of Jesus transfigured, witness the arrival of the cloud and, from it, the voice of God affirming that Jesus is his Son. Now is the time to listen to what the Son is explaining about life, living, suffering and death. Only by listening attentively to Jesus' teaching will what he is making known be fully understood when he appears to them all again, in just a few weeks' time in the glory of his resurrection state.

As the fifteenth-century German philosopher Nicholas of Cusa suggests in *On Learned Ignorance*, perception is crucial: 'Led in learned ignorance to the mountain that is Christ ... we come, as in a thinner cloud, to perceive him more clearly.' What we are in fact witnesses to on the holy mountain this Lent is the clearest, most emphatic communication from God in the New Testament. Here is Jesus. Please stop talking. Listen to him.

Today's Thought: Think of one epiphany 'penny dropping' moment in your own life for which you want to give thanks this Lent?

28

Tuesday: Voice

Distinctive Voices

We turn our attention now to the voice that speaks from the cloud.

Everyone has a distinct voice. It is part of our uniqueness as individuals. Once in the actual broadcast studio of BBC Radio 4's *Today* programme to present *Thought for the Day*, there are often a few minutes before the slot goes live as it is in the context of the wider news and current affairs programme. I love listening to the vast array of specialist voices on a range of subjects – natural history, politics, literature, art, science. This is why radio is my preferred medium. The voice is everything.

I had a very strange experience recently when officiating at a school Christmas carol service in Olympia, West London. Afterwards, a young mum whose child had been taking part asked me if I had officiated at a funeral of one of her own young classmates 30 years earlier. 'As soon as I heard your voice,' she told me, 'I knew it was you and I want you to know that I still remember what you said after our tragic loss.' I was seriously humbled and amazed that she recognized me by my voice. It is true, of course, that our voices are uniquely ours – they are an intrinsic part of our personalities and partly make us who we are.

In the Hebrew scriptures, the voice of God is heard occasionally and, when it is, it is often also identifiable because of the vehicle by which God sometimes appears on the scene – namely via a cloud. In the garden of Eden (Genesis 3.8), God's voice spreads panic or fear because the sound of it is synonymous with judgement. When God delivers the Ten Commandments to Moses in Exodus 20, the tone of the divine voice is direct and authoritative. Psalm 29 describes God's voice poetically in several of its verses. Read verses 3–9 of this psalm especially, even just for the poetry, and enjoy many such examples.

As Lenten pilgrims on the Transfiguration mountain, we recall the clarity and authority of God making his purposes known to his people in the Old Testament. But whether via the messages of angels in communicating Jesus' future birth to Mary or the shepherds after his birth – or again, via an angel, to Joseph warning the holy family to leave by another way to avoid Herod, and to those who witnessed Jesus' baptism when a similar cloud and voice affirm God's pleasure directly in his Son – the message of the voice of God is different as we arrive at this *epiphany* moment of the Transfiguration. In a world of noise, much of which is worrying and concerning, God's voice says to each pilgrim, 'Draw away, just for a little while, to regain a sense of perspective. Look at the radiant person of Jesus and listen to him.' As the Transfiguration story in 2 Peter outlines, this voice comes 'from the Majestic Glory' from which the apostles 'heard this voice that came from heaven'. We gaze at the cloud, hearing the voice. The need is simply to listen.

Today's Thought: In what ways would you say that you have heard the voice of God during your own life pilgrimage so far?

29

Wednesday: Baptism

Two of a Kind

We have so far seen real similarities between the baptism and Transfiguration stories in the Bible. They are two of a kind. In both, there is a cloud, a voice and a clear message from God. As part of today's reflection, you might find it useful to have a look at the three baptism stories in Mark 1.9–11, Matthew 3.13–17 and Luke 3.21–22, in the same way that we considered the various accounts of the Transfiguration before setting out.

You will see then that the message spoken by God's voice to those looking on as Jesus is baptized is key here. In the same way as on the mountain, by the River Jordan a cloud appears and the voice comes from the cloud with the message: 'This is my Son, whom I Love; with him I am well pleased.' There is no imperative however to listen as on the mountain top. Instead, a statement of satisfaction and delight between Father and Son is spoken.

As Easter approaches, one of the highlights of the season is to be invited to renew our baptism vows. This rite at Easter emphasizes how baptism is a sign of our membership of the Christian family as, together, we renew our promises and reaffirm our commitment. Baptism is the sacrament of joining and of renewal, of being washed clean and starting over afresh. We are marked in oil with the cross of Jesus, with the water symbolizing the defeat of death and resurrection to eternal life.

In his various letters, St Paul refers to the transformation brought about when a believer is baptized. The whole language of the baptism service is one of transformation. The old is put away and the newly baptized puts on the new life brought about in the transforming powers of the waters of baptism. There is a lot of language in the Epistles about the contrast between life before and after baptism (see Galatians 3.27 and Ephesians 4.22–25).

Even if we are not always aware of it, the significance of our own baptism is constantly revised and reframed as life moves on and we mature as Christians. We can never be sure where baptism leads us, but once baptized it remains for ever part of who we are. Indeed, we then continue a pilgrim journey with all of its ups and downs and twists and turns. Clement of Alexandria writes: 'Being baptised, we are enlightened; being enlightened, we are adopted as children; being adopted, we are made perfect; being made complete, we are made immortal.'

As we consider the symbol of the cloud throughout this section, the similarities between the baptism and Transfiguration stories become increasingly obvious as far as God's entrance on the scene is concerned. Both are present when Jesus begins his public ministry in Galilee. Both are also present on the mountain top as Jesus prepares for the culmination of his work. Enjoy reading and reflecting on the baptism stories again as we thank God (those of us who have been baptized) for our own baptism.

Today's Thought: Give thanks to God for those who brought you to baptism and pray for fresh understanding of that moment in your life.

30

Thursday: Listening

If We Do Not Listen, We Do Not Come to the Truth

Having established that the message of the divine voice on the summit of the mountain was an imperative, a command to listen to what Jesus is saying, we should perhaps now also consider what are the consequences of God's command for us as modern-day pilgrims. On Tuesday we recognized that, even with all the background Hebrew teaching concerning the voice, there is no going back from our vantage point on the mountain: rather, the command from the voice concerns our future and the world's future going forward in terms of suffering, death and resurrection.

It's interesting to look more closely at the three Gospel accounts of the Transfiguration again as far as the actual message of the voice is concerned: here are the words of the divine voice, translated from the Greek:

Mark: 'This is my Son, whom I love. Listen to him!'
Luke: 'This is my Son, whom I have chosen; listen to him.'
Matthew: 'This is my Son, whom I love; with him I am well pleased. Listen to him!'

The accounts are very similar. Mark and Matthew additionally suggest that God declares his love. Matthew adds that God is happy with Jesus. Luke further emphasizes that Jesus is the chosen one as far as the Father is concerned.

Lent is surely a good time in the Christian year to do a bit more listening. We ask God, Father, Son and Holy Spirit, through a variety of spiritual disciplines, that we may be open to the Lord's promptings. Our task, on any pilgrim journey, is to discern how we pray for those things that need changing in our world and lives, or what we would like to change for the better. We undergird our ability and willingness to listen to God because we know this is a reciprocal act: God is also listening to us. Hence our listening is part of a conversation involving being open to God in a variety of ways. Offering thoughts and prayers and petitions to him while, at the same time, listening to the Son whom God has chosen and loves – this is the imperative.

The English Benedictine monk Hubert van Zeller, in *The Mystery of Suffering*, says, 'If we do not listen, we do not come to the truth. If we do not pray, we do not even get as far as listening.' I love this quote because it deals with the presumptions we make self-consciously about discerning the truth, listening and what the life of prayer is all about. Jesus is declared Son of God on Mount Tabor emphatically by God and then goes on to reveal his Father's glory. All that has gone before, all those Old Testament utterances of the voice of God, is now framed on the Transfiguration mountain. We gaze and admire the scene; but to come to the truth, the task is always a listening one. To listen we must always attend to our lives of prayer.

Today's Thought: We have two ears and one mouth – perhaps so we can listen twice as much as we speak?

31

Friday: Son of God

The Son of God is the One Who is Raised from the Dead

The various titles used of Jesus by himself, others and the Gospel writers have been the source of a great deal of analysis and reflection. What does each of them mean? On the mountain top, various titles are attributed to Jesus in different places within the three Gospel accounts, but it is clear that 'Son of God' and 'Son of Man' are the most important. It is worth noting that only Jesus uses the title Son of Man about himself. It is also often summarized that Son of Man best relates to Jesus' humanity whereas Son of God refers to his divine status.

In both the baptism and Transfiguration stories, Jesus is declared Son of God directly by the Father. Bringing all three Gospel accounts together, God seems to be saying, in total: 'This is my son, whom I have chosen, whom I love and with whom I am well pleased. Listen to him!' The divine vindication of the Son with a consequent imperative is made clear to us as viewers of the scene.

Some scholars believe that the title 'Son of God' sits better when used after the resurrection. While it is rarely used before Easter, after the resurrection, 'Son of God' certainly seems to become the most important title used of Jesus in the early Church. It is the Son who overcomes death, triumphs through his resurrection and ascends to his Father in glory. But more than that, just as we are called to be obedient to the call of Jesus through our baptism, our Lord is also called to the same obedience in fulfilling the will of his Father through his glorious passion and death on the cross. On the mountain that we witness as pilgrims this Lent, the Son of God is momentarily seen in a way that will only finally be revealed after the events of Good Friday have taken place: a glorious Son to whom we must listen.

The series of unfolding events surrounding the Transfiguration have come to a climax here. They are principally about revealing Jesus' identity and his unique relationship with his Father. God affirms Jesus as his Son and in the book of Acts, the Epistles and in the writings of the early Church, the beloved Son is seen on the holy mountain to reflect the glory that the world longs for.

The cloud appears. The voice speaks. A command is issued. It is God the Father who identifies the Son whom he has chosen and whom he loves. We are to listen to the Son who will soon reveal the extent of his love for us as Jesus enters Jerusalem for the final time in his earthly state.

Of course, the disciples are to remain quiet for now, even after a glimpse of the future has been revealed. But their time will come, and so will ours, as Easter beckons. It is to an obedience to the Father's command that we too are called this Lent.

Today's Thought: How do you see the title Son of God when you think of the whole gospel story? Is it a title of Jesus that you like?

32

Saturday: Doubt

Below the Level

We are all affected by doubt from time to time. Some more than others, of course. Bishop Richard Chartres said once in a podcast that doubt is not the opposite of faith because the opposite of faith is life turned in on itself. Learning to shun doubt and to be a faithful disciple is a daily challenge. The more we learn, the more we realize how easy it is to trip up and fail. Our understanding in terms of faith is limited. Faith is a lifelong journey.

Discovering who Jesus is and what that involves in our daily lives is both exciting and challenging. There was no going back for the disciples after Peter had confessed Jesus as Messiah at Caesarea Philippi, but that did not mean that it was all clear sailing from this point. The Transfiguration, the cloud, the divine voice, all in the presence of Moses and Elijah, the tabernacles suggestion – all this leaves the disciples with plenty of further food for thought. But Jesus' command to silence and the hugely challenging itinerary that awaited them down below in the valley posed problems, which failed to deal completely with the doubt that raised its head from time to time.

The denial of Jesus by Peter in the courtyard is perhaps the most dramatic example of this (Matthew 26.69–75). In view of what has just taken place on Mount Tabor, is it not staggering that Peter had the temerity to deny even knowing Jesus, when he had confessed him as Lord at Caesarea and seen the glory revealed on the mountain? And yet, we do understand. Being told to keep the whole thing a secret is just an additional pressure. Doubt affects us all. It is never far from the surface and manifests itself variously. We can and do often identify with Peter here.

Every year, in Holy Week, we cannot but be absorbed by Jesus' vulnerability to the extremes of human sinfulness and violence while, at the same time, being reassured deep within ourselves that the path of suffering inevitably leads to the glory just revealed. And it is true that in our digital world it is self-belief and self-gratification that seem to be the dominating priorities with regard to how people behave. Many younger people seem happy in their isolated worlds, not perhaps realizing how what is happening now in the present inevitably, in part, frames their future. Belief systems which have sustained civilizations for generations are increasingly under threat because people are living for the moment without a thought for the future.

In modern society we hear a lot about doubt. And we have been through a great deal: the pandemic, economic challenges, recent conflicts in Europe and further afield. The pilgrim journey against such a background throws up daily questions and challenges. Ever the optimist, in his last ever BBC *Thought for the Day*, the late former Chief Rabbi Jonathan Sacks urged his listeners to try not to be overcome by doubt. I leave you with his faithful words below.

Today's Thought: 'We have been through too much simply to go back to where we were. We have to rescue some blessings from the curse, some hope from the pain' (Jonathan Sacks).

A Prayer

Glory to You, Christ our God, who appeared and enlightened the world. Today, You appeared to the world, and Your light, O Lord, has left its mark upon us as in fuller understanding we sing to You: 'You came, You were made manifest, the unapproachable light.'

(An Orthodox prayer)

Questions

What role does your baptism play in your sense of Christian formation? How do you regard it from where you are now?

Are you a talker or a listener or a bit of both?

'Doubting Thomas' is still used often as a phrase to sum people up. How do you deal with doubt in your own life and faith?

The Fifth Sunday of Lent – Glory

'The Transfiguration shows us how Jesus transforms us and the whole of creation with his dazzling light. It is a scene that holds together promise and fulfilment, cross and resurrection, earth and heaven, time and eternity.'

(Philip North, Bishop of Blackburn)

33

Sunday: Passiontide

A Lifelong Pilgrimage

The last two weeks of Lent are still often referred to as Passiontide. Lent deepens. Expectation rises. We move up a gear in our journey towards the cross of Jesus. The inevitability of his suffering and death somehow becomes more urgent and apparent. So, in these days before Holy Week, we examine the nub of the Transfiguration story in the context of Jesus' passion.

The visible consequences of Jesus' Transfiguration are stunningly bright. The immediate effects include an intensity of the stark whiteness, which we will explore in more detail. It is in real contrast to the earthiness and blue sky dominating the mountainous venue, as we saw in the Transfiguration icon.

The two central themes or motifs emanating from Jesus' actual Transfiguration are *doxa* (glory) and *light*. These words, each of which has significant theological weight, implore us to consider God's vindication of the suffering of his Son. Participating as pilgrims in Jesus' passion ensures that we are also able to share in the eternal light promised in the resurrection when the darkness of the world is pierced and overcome once and for all.

Today, Passion Sunday, we visualize the intensity of the story that unfolds throughout next week. We prepare for it outwardly and drink in what it means inwardly to have the strength to face whatever life holds for us on our individual journeys. Having faith in the glory revealed by Jesus, and looking always to the radiant light beyond a world of darkness, is not limited to Passiontide. It is a daily challenge, as we were reminded at the start of this journey. Every day is a transfiguration day as we pray for God's transforming power. Reminding ourselves of this often demands all our inner strength. We are easily weighed down by life's challenges. We need to hold on to the vision.

When I first worked in London in the 1990s, Cardinal Basil Hume was the leader of the Catholic Church in Britain. I was honoured to meet him on several occasions. There is now a magnificent statue of him outside Newcastle Central Station near to the city's Catholic cathedral. Whenever I see it, I remember him explaining how sharing in Jesus' passion was a lifelong pilgrimage, undertaken stage by stage, at different levels. He acknowledged that 'At times there can be periods of stress and strain, periods of sadness and sorrow, in which we truly are living the Passion of Christ in our lives.'

For us to share in the glory embodied in our transfigured Lord, suffering with him is not an option. One of the toughest things about the Christian life is to accept and live with the reality of suffering. But living the passion of Christ daily in our lives also means keeping our eyes fixed on the radiancy of his glory, not losing sight of it. Jesus' overcoming of both individual suffering and the suffering of the world is based on the sacrifice he is about to make, which is the foundation stone of what our Lord has done for us. It is for that reason that we have first been given this vision of glory.

Today's Thought: Isn't Cardinal Hume right when he suggests that faith demands that we remain faithful even when the going is particularly tough?

34

Monday: Metamorphosis

Lasting Change

I was proud that my local church where I grew up in Hull was called the Church of the Transfiguration. There are so few of them in the UK, it made us feel very special. But we always had a problem. 'Transfiguration? What on earth is that?' people would say, followed quickly by, 'Why name a church after such a strange event?'

Jesus is described as *metamorphosed* in Mark and Matthew, but Luke omits the verb. It describes a dramatic, profound change in Jesus. In the ancient world (for example, in Greek and Roman society), people were often described as being dramatically changed all the time into different kinds of beings and creatures. Apart from Moses on Mount Sinai (Exodus 34.29–35), however, such a change as we witness here in Jesus is unprecedented in the Bible.

But what was transfigured? Was it Jesus' whole person? Or just his clothes? Or his face and his clothes? Look at the various accounts again and you will note the variations on a theme. In his classic commentary on Mark's Gospel, D. E. Nineham suggests,

> The idea seems to be that Jesus temporarily exchanged the normal human form that he bore during his earthly life for that glorious form he was believed to possess after his exaltation to heaven, and which believers also hoped to be clothed with after his second coming.

As Holy Week approaches, I suggest we identify three clear phases of Jesus' existence which might help guide us through the days ahead: the *earthly* Son of Man who shares our humanity; the *risen* Son of God who fulfils God's promise of new life; and the *radiant* Saviour of the world who is seated at the right hand of God beyond the resurrection.

Jesus has already promised that he would go ahead of us to heaven to prepare a place for us. What is more, in the face of present-day suffering here, our hearts are not to be troubled or afraid. This is easier said than lived out, but is the challenge of true discipleship.

There are undoubtedly many things in our lives that we would like to change. In the wider world, in the Church and in our daily existence, there are hurdles needing to be overcome so that the glory of God can be seen more brightly. The verb *to transfigure* is key to understanding *how* on the holy mountain Jesus shows us the way and *why* the Transfiguration, offered here after centuries of waiting, is revelatory, radical and potentially life changing.

I personally believe there is nothing God cannot change. The transfiguration of all suffering is the greatest promise to us. As Bishop Philip North says in the quote at the start of this section, Mount Tabor is 'a scene that holds together promise and fulfilment, cross and resurrection, earth and heaven, time and eternity'.

Today's Thought: Have you ever been dazzled by light – maybe the early morning sun or a beam from a car? What words would you use to describe that kind of light and its effects on you?

35

Tuesday: Transfiguration White

His Face Shone Like the Sun

If a paint manufacturer were to launch a new white paint and call it transfiguration white, what might it look like? On a colour card of a current leading paint producer, I can choose between *absolute* white, *morning* light, *Jasmine* white and *pure brilliant* white, not to mention *frosted dawn*, *cliff walk* and *timeless*. But what about transfiguration white? How might it look?

I have already explained how, as a result of the metamorphosis of Jesus, his appearance changes and whiteness dominates the scene. Mark describes Jesus' clothes as 'dazzling white', while Luke adds that his face, and the faces of Moses and Elijah, share his glorious radiancy. Matthew adds that Jesus' face shone like the sun and his clothes become white as light. Some will remember a famous soap powder television advert – how the filthy, muddy clothes were transformed into pure whiteness. Here on the mountain, a small, select audience witness Jesus as he has never been seen before and, from an earthly perspective, never will be again.

Transfiguration white, as revealed on the holy mountain, is a direct consequence of the dramatic change that takes place. It is also the colour most associated with the glory of God. It represents the light of the world, in stark contrast to the darkness which the glory challenges at every turn, and which also points to the glory of the resurrection.

The exciting and dramatic seventh chapter of the book of Revelation, the last book in the Bible, contains a number of clues as to what the future might look like. A great multitude is assembled. And, for sure, they are all wearing white robes. 'What are these which are arrayed in white robes? and whence came they?' asks one of the elders in verse 13. The answer follows in verse 14: 'These are they which came out of the great tribulation, and have washed their robes and made them white in the blood of the lamb' (KJV).

The connection here between Jesus the sacrificial lamb and the white robes of those who have been saved takes us back to everything we said earlier on this pilgrimage about our baptism into Christ. The whiteness displayed before the disciples and ourselves on the mountain also underlines that we have already passed to new life through the waters of death.

White is also the liturgical colour used in baptism services. It is a symbol of celebration, festivities, joyfulness and hope. For us today it represents the future glory of the Father which, on the mountain, overcomes the darkness of the world. Once again, it is through baptism that we are called to live this life of transformation and to share it with others.

Today's Thought: Try to describe the nearest thing you can think of that might be transfiguration white.

36

Wednesday: Doxa

We Have Seen His Glory

Perhaps no word in the Bible has a more fascinating history than the word 'glory', which in Greek is *doxa* and *kavod* in Hebrew. However, in the Greek translation of the Old Testament, known as the Septuagint, the same word is used to translate both *kavod* and the Aramaic word *shekinah*. *Shekinah* is right out of a transfiguration textbook because it suggests God dwelling among his people, as in the tabernacle. Ramsey underlines this in his classic work *The Glory of God and the Transfiguration of Christ*, 'The Septuagint sets the imagery of glory, tabernacle and the dwelling of [the Lord] in a composite pattern.' In other words, they are perfectly brought together.

Only Luke uses the word *doxa* in his version of the Transfiguration story. As a Gentile, he must have been aware of the extraordinary significance the word had for his audience on multiple levels. Luke is attempting to sum up the whole vision here in terms of fulfilment. Today, Christians still frequently recall God's glory in worship. From the Gloria in the Eucharist and the conclusion of the communal singing or saying of psalms and canticles. we continuously proclaim this *doxa*.

A chain reaction emerges here: the Transfiguration results in a display of intense whiteness, interpreted as God's glory, which is reflected elsewhere, particularly in St John's Gospel, as the light of the world.

We know that the Transfiguration challenges us to believe that there is nothing that God cannot change through faith. And that the whiteness also recalls our baptism as witnesses of Jesus' sacrifice on the cross leading us through the waters of death to the glory and light we contemplate today – the *kavod*, the *shekinah*, the *doxa*, the glory.

If St John's is the Gospel of glory, where the word *doxa* appears often, it is a surprise that John omits the Transfiguration altogether. We will reflect on this more during Eastertide. In John's introduction, known as the Prologue, we read, 'We have seen his glory, the glory of the one and only Son, who came from the Father, full of grace and truth' (1.14). The vision of glory on Mount Tabor is reassuring both to Jesus' friends on the mountain and the Church today and would not be out of place in the Fourth Gospel.

In her book *The Transfiguration*, the scholar Dorothy Lee suggests that, in Luke, glory 'symbolises the celestial abode to which the mountain gives access and also the divine permanence that embraces Jesus.' It is clear that Jesus belongs at the same time to both the earthly and heavenly realms. The past is brought into the present on the mountain and the epiphany then points to the future. Jesus is transfigured. We keep on recalling in Lent and every day that there is nothing God cannot change. We are bathed in white as we prepare for our Lord's passion. We behold his glory here, full of grace and truth. And, at the same time, this *doxa* reflects the divine light which pierces the darkness that surrounds us.

Today's Thought: Glory to the Father, and to the Son, and to the Holy Spirit. As it was in the beginning, is now and ever shall be, world without end. Amen.

37

Thursday: Light

The Hour Has Come

Jesus is transfigured. The scene is bathed in white. This unique transfiguration white reflects the glory of God in which the newly baptized are bathed. The offering of a lighted candle to the newly baptized at the end of a baptism service is a significant moment indeed.

Light is a persistent and constant theme throughout the Bible. From creation, through the books known as the Wisdom literature (including many references in the psalms), light is usually a sign of God's presence. It is in stark contrast to the bleak darkness often affecting the world (sin, despondency and despair).

To explore more fully the connection between glory and light, I suggest spending some time contemplating John 12.20–end. When we later consider some of the possible reasons for St John's omission of the Transfiguration story, this passage offers a further glimpse of an already profound analysis of what the light revealed on the mountain top means both for the cosmos and for every believer.

Some Greeks attending a festival ask Philip if they can see Jesus. Philip relays this to Andrew, and the two pass on the message to Jesus. A critical verse (v. 23) is when Jesus declares, probably somewhat to the surprise of Philip and Andrew, 'The hour has come for the Son of Man to be glorified.' In a very short sentence, we have confirmation of the imminence of Jesus' passion, the use of the title 'Son of Man' (which we turn to next as it is inextricably linked to Jesus' death and passion), as well as a direct reference to the overall consequences of all of this:

the glorification of the Son of Man. A few verses later (v. 28), Jesus prays directly to God: 'Father, glorify your name!'

The crowd, acting as our representatives in a way, later ask, 'Who is this Son of Man?' before the intriguing reference to the writings of the prophet Isaiah where, to put it simply, the people repeatedly fail to recognize God's glory. Jesus is clear that any 'lessons learnt exercise' involves a clear recognition of the connection between suffering, glory and light.

As if to spell this out even more clearly, Jesus says: 'I have come into the world as a light, so that no one who believes in me should stay in darkness' (v. 46), which for the crowd listening is probably as clear, if not as mysterious, as it could be. Earlier, also uniquely in John (chapter 8), Jesus declares, 'I am the light of the world.' This theme links the light with his imminent suffering and future glory. Indeed, it is so developed and understood in John's Gospel that he is continually explaining the significance of what happened on Mount Tabor without recounting the story itself. The light has come into a world in a new and totally transforming way: and his name is Jesus.

Today's Thought: Have you ever experienced complete darkness and then been able to see the glory of a starlit night? Describe the feeling for a moment.

38

Friday: Son of Man

Hidden Reality

As I mentioned when we reflected on the title Son of God, no one else in the Gospels uses the title 'Son of Man' of Jesus except Jesus himself. Why? Jesus uses Son of Man on a total of 80 occasions, suggesting it is the name he felt was highly appropriate and perfectly summed up his mission. The number of references to the title are as follows: Matthew (32), Mark (14), Luke (26) and John (10). In all three Gospels where the Transfiguration is described, the title Son of Man is used both before and after the events on the mountain top.

Mark writes that, 'As they were coming down the mountain, Jesus gave them orders not to tell anyone what they had seen until the Son of Man had risen from the dead. They kept the matter to themselves, discussing what "rising from the dead" meant.' In Matthew, the last thing Jesus says before the Transfiguration is, 'Truly I tell you, some who are standing here will not taste death before they see the Son of Man coming in his kingdom' (16.28), while at the conclusion of the Transfiguration, the evangelist reports the same conversation as Mark.

Between the already talked about conversation at Caesarea Philippi and the Transfiguration, Luke reports that Jesus 'strictly warned them not to tell this to anyone ... "The Son of Man must suffer many things and be rejected by the elders, the chief priests and the teachers of the law, and he must be killed and on the third day be raised to life"' (9.21–22). It is easy to conclude that the title 'Son of Man' really is of great significance to Jesus and his own understanding of the essential nature of his mission on behalf of the Father.

When considering the title 'Son of God', I suggested it was too simplistic to say that 'Son of Man' refers to Jesus' *human* nature while 'Son of God' reflects his *divine* status. But Jesus' dual status as God and human is never far from the surface when these titles are being used and they are mutually complementary across a wide range of contexts.

Even in the writings of the early Church Fathers, as the historian Boniface Ramsey in *Beginning to Read the Fathers* explains, it is as both Son of Man and Son of God that Jesus has the power to effect the change and transfiguration that his mission reveals to the faithful: 'Perhaps the most striking and prevalent characterisation of this dynamic understanding of Christ, which finds a kind of culmination in his suffering and death, is that of transformation.'

The Transfiguration marks a crucial stage in the disciples' pilgrimage and their understanding of who Jesus is. For us as pilgrims today, we are surely comfortable with the idea that we have the Son of Man who, after his suffering, will finally be unveiled at the resurrection as Son of God. As Pope Benedict majestically puts it in *Jesus of Nazareth*: 'It fits exactly with the method of Jesus' preaching, in as much as he spoke in riddles and parables so as to lead gradually to the hidden reality that can truly be discovered only through discipleship.'

Today's Thought: Think of one of those moments in your life which you would describe as key – a point from which there was no going back. What was going on?

39

Saturday: Descent

It's Inevitable

When I first studied the Transfiguration at Sheffield University, there was one phrase that has always stuck in my mind. I believe it was Professor Morna Hooker who coined the phrase that, after Mount Tabor, it was 'all downhill to Jerusalem after that'. Whatever else I have read on the subject over many years, this is one key phrase I have kept coming back to. The party arrives at the summit. Great events happen. But then the return journey is inevitable.

I've already mentioned a verse of the Transfiguration hymn 'Tis good Lord to be here' which plays on Peter's response to the scene. With regards to the inevitable descent to reality, the world as we know it, the words of another verse of the same hymn declare,

> 'Tis good Lord to be here!
> Yet we may not remain;
> But since you bid us leave the mount,
> Come with us to the plain.

We have also already stressed over again the important point that Jesus tells the disciples not to say anything until after the resurrection. The descent did not mean that they could talk openly about the epiphany that they had seen on the mountain top. The opposite was true. They could say nothing for now. The secret of Jesus' messiahship must stay hidden for the time being.

Over many years, I have preached on the theme of a return to the valley after the tumultuous events on the mountain top. After a glimpse of Jesus' real identity and the witnessing of the glory in such dramatic fashion, it cannot have been easy to return to the reality and challenges of what everyday life had been like before, albeit from a new perspective. Of course, they would never forget the mountain-top experience. It framed everything else that followed. But in a practical sense, faced with increasing animosity and cynicism from the religious authorities of the day, it was to the inevitability of the cross that Jesus' attention turned. Neither he nor his followers were to be afraid because of what lay ahead. That, however, was easier said than done, as St Peter in the courtyard has already reminded us.

Most people experience that feeling of dread at some point in their life – the facing of the music, the moment of truth, the meeting or encounter that just must be faced whether we like it or not. The idea that 'I would just like to stay here for a while longer and not go home' or 'Here I am safer than I will ever be anywhere else' is a common experience, whether people have faith or not.

Facing this descent demands stoicism, fortitude and courage. While the disciples do not yet fully understand the enormity of what they have just witnessed on the mountain, the descent to reality must nevertheless have been a challenging one. They probably gathered all their strength, prepared themselves for the inevitable question, and played over and over in their heads and hearts that the implications of the summit experience were for life back down below.

Today's Thought: When are you at your happiest and what is it about those moments that you never want to end?

A Prayer

Christ is that Morning Star which, when the night of this age shall be past, brings to his saints the promised light of life, and opens the everlasting Day.
Amen.

(The Venerable Bede)

Questions

What would you most like to change in your own life at the present time, and why?

White is a fascinating colour. Why do you think it best represents God's glory?

Talking of 'seeing the light' says lots of different things to different people. How do you see it?

Holy Week –
Transfiguration of Suffering

'For me the Transfiguration means that Jesus reveals his own glorious eternal heavenly destiny – and in doing so he reveals mine too! The way to get there is not to seek a life of mountain-top euphoria but to follow Jesus on the costly path of suffering: to Jerusalem and to the cross.'

(Ruth Bushyager, Bishop of Horsham)

40

Palm Sunday: Palm Cross

Hosannah!

At the various churches where I have ministered, it has always been a privilege to serve on Palm Sunday morning. Whatever the weather, a heap of freshly blessed palm crosses is received by the faithful from a ceremonial plate with deep gratitude. Processions usually follow during the singing of the hymn 'All glory, laud and honour'. We hear afresh the story of Holy Week, often in dramatic form, as pilgrims hold their palm crosses in their hands.

The eight days of Holy Week, beginning today, are the most profound of the Christian year. The atmosphere at the time of Jesus was tense around occupied Jerusalem. We can sense the feeling for Jesus, his disciples and his wider family and friends as a mood of inevitability surrounds the holy city. It is Passover too. Both the Roman and Jewish authorities would have been aware that Jesus was approaching the city. There would have been a variety of views on how to deal with this extraordinary figure from Galilee.

In this section we focus inevitably on the connection between Mount Tabor and the hill known as Golgotha. One is a high and lonely Galilean mountain suggesting glory and radiance; the other a lonely, forbidding Jerusalem hill, symbolizing cruelty and execution. Together, these two contrasting hills bring together for Holy Week the combined themes of suffering and glory.

Palm Sunday is a day to reflect on suffering: the suffering of the world in general and of those close to us, and indeed our own suffering, might all be at the forefront of our minds. It is a moment also for intense honesty. There are many questions to face.

Over the next few days, the Church absorbs significant and momentous symbols that make Holy Week so extraordinary. Special services often take place daily, focusing on particular themes and aspects of the final days of Jesus' earthly life. It is also a week for Chrism (the blessing of oils), the washing of feet, thanksgiving for the Eucharist, of vigils and following the stations of the cross. Christians mark Good Friday in a variety of ways, not least by venerating the cross of Christ and praying that the glory revealed on Mount Tabor might now be for ever present in the darkness which is so extreme that it is easy to lose hope. The convergence of eternal light and life through the deep darkness of death is ever more apparent.

Our palm crosses are symbols of all of this. They help us to keep focused on the bigger picture. God speaks again through the passion and cross of Jesus. Our task is to remember the divine imperative and to listen.

Pope Francis, in a Good Friday address, said that the cross of Jesus 'is the word through which God has responded to evil in the world'. He conceded that sometimes it seems as if the world's evil goes unchecked and that God is silent, 'and yet, God has spoken, he has replied, and his answer to the cross of Christ: a word which is love, mercy, forgiveness'. We make this journey through Holy Week not alone but as one of a great company of pilgrims sharing together in the wonder of what Jesus is about to do for us.

Today's Thought: Take your most recent palm cross or any cross and reflect on it as the greatest symbol of light in darkness.

41

Monday: Suffering

Golgotha Approaches

Why do people suffer? It's possibly the question I'm asked most as a priest. It is also always at the back of my mind when I write scripts for BBC's *Thought for the Day*: how to account for limitless direct and indirect suffering following a national or international atrocity, natural disaster or terrible accident? They are always the most difficult scripts to write. Apart from welcome 'thoughts and prayers', what else can one say?

To rationalize suffering of any kind from a theological point of view is a complex issue. There is no point taking an easy way out. We surely accept that suffering exists at various levels and through different means. Natural disasters, the existence of disease in an imperfect creation, as well as human sinfulness, are among the obvious catalysts or causes of suffering. In the Hebrew scriptures, many rhetorical questions are still asked, particularly in the writings of the prophets and in the wisdom literature, as to why a God of love and compassion would allow such things.

It is my view, after decades of reflecting on the Transfiguration story, that this is, in a way, suffering's *once and for all* moment. Aware of what was about to befall him, Jesus takes his three friends away from it all to put suffering into a proper perspective and to show the world a way through it. This Holy Week, the intrinsic connection between suffering and glory is key to understanding how Jesus the Saviour literally saves us from our sinfulness. What is more, this is done even on the mountain in the context of prayer. They were surely praying that the world's darkness would be pierced by the light of his glory in which suffering is no more. This is a lot to digest and absorb. It is also key to our Easter hope and the victory we will soon proclaim over death itself.

By being willing to accept the terrible suffering of his crucifixion, Jesus presents his passion as a way through which suffering can be transformed. After his Transfiguration, we have Jesus' resurrection and ascension, along with a promise of even more to come. The Second Coming of Jesus is a huge subject, but the expectancy that Jesus will return at some point in the future to complete the transformation has been part of the Church's expectation for centuries.

My young grandson reminded me how as children we are so easily scared of things. We don't like monsters and villains. We like to know that the good guy will win out in the end. He has taught me how a perfect world might look if only I had the faith of a child again. It is a beautiful thing to behold. But we adults know that, as we get older, life is more and more complicated and we become absorbed in all sorts of complexities, often causing hurt and suffering for others. If we want to deal with suffering, we know the costly path we are challenged to follow. Ruth Bushyager, Bishop of Horsham, stresses in the quote at the beginning of this section how we need 'not to seek a life of mountain-top euphoria but to follow Jesus on the costly path of suffering: to Jerusalem and to the cross'. This is a reality to grasp gratefully as Holy Week continues.

Today's Thought: How does the story of the Transfiguration help your own understanding of suffering in the world?

42

Tuesday: Loneliness

Remembering Sheila

Surveys reveal that at least a quarter of people feel lonely at some time in their lives. The pandemic certainly highlighted the causes and consequences of loneliness. But loneliness has always been prevalent in society.

It also affects all parts of the community. While it can be heightened in isolated rural areas, it is also experienced in highly populated places where the lonely can be even more hidden. I have served in parishes as varied as Central and East London, the Yorkshire Dales and now in Welwyn Garden City. I know that loneliness is a factor wherever people live.

It also affects people of all ages. While many young people might be in touch with each other digitally, physical isolation from peers is a reality for many young adults. After the birth of a child, young parents also can find it difficult to connect with others. It is true too that isolation can be experienced when acting as the principal carer of a family member affected by dementia, bereavement or old age. We need to be honest: it is too easy to be lonely.

Sheila Seleoane was found dead in her London flat more than two years after she had died alone. The housing association responsible for her accommodation, the police and other authorities missed numerous opportunities to find her. Her neighbours were distraught that they had not been able to do more. It resulted in a national debate as to what can be done to reduce the number of people who experience loneliness.

During Holy Week we might ponder how lonely and isolated those close to Jesus must have felt. His mother Mary and the other women, Peter and the remaining disciples, all who knew and were acquainted with Jesus, saw with despair what had befallen him and felt helpless to do anything. They were increasingly isolated and eventually locked themselves away, cut off from the outside world.

On the cross, Jesus obviously felt total dereliction and a sense of being on his own: 'My God, my God, why have you forsaken me?' (Mark 15.34). This is a cry from the heart from the Son of Man at a moment of deepest pain and darkness. The light seemed to have been extinguished. Jesus' isolation and loneliness gives way to silence. For a few hours between Friday and early on Sunday morning there is complete emptiness with only a hint of expectation because of what we know then followed.

Being a good neighbour does not mean being overbearing or nosey. There is nothing worse! It does, however, demand that we look out for the isolated and lonely in our communities and try to be beacons of light to those who might be finding it difficult because they feel cut off and afraid. A friendly word, a knock on the door, the offer of a cup of tea or a walk if you feel someone is isolated and simply needs company can work wonders. Holy Week is undoubtedly a time to see if there is some way to bring even a small amount of light into the lives of others.

Today's Thought: Are you a good neighbour? How can we all do more to combat loneliness?

43

Wednesday: Don't Say a Word!

Finding Words for Mystery

Some are better at keeping secrets than others. Particularly when under pressure. Sometimes, of course, people say, 'Please don't tell anyone,' with the obvious intention of wanting others to know anyway. That can be tricky. But when someone decides that they have a level of trust and understanding with another person and can confide in them, this is usually a good thing, and the emphasis is on the confidant to keep silent and be there for that person.

Several times already on this pilgrimage we have reflected on Jesus' command to silence in the Gospels. There are lots of examples of miracles and signs after which Jesus issues such an instruction. Like us, when we are told something we think should or might be better shared, the disciples must have thought, 'Why are we not allowed to say a word about everything he is telling us?'

The most obvious conclusion is that the purpose of the miracle or sign was, for the moment, for those who witnessed it. In terms of keeping things a secret for the time being, Jesus possibly wanted the disciples to have more insights and the bigger picture rather than a series of isolated incidents. He was concerned about the pressure the disciples might be put under by the authorities as the situation became more tense. In Mark and Matthew, Jesus gives them 'orders' not to say anything about the glory on the mountain until they had witnessed the resurrection. Luke reports, 'the disciples kept this to themselves and did not tell anyone at that time what they had seen'.

Rowan Williams, in *Meeting God in Mark*, does not mince his words when considering the human weakness of Jesus' friends in not understanding why the kingdom needed to be kept a secret. Peter, as we have stressed, was afraid on the mountain and did not know what to say. But Williams believes this was more because they realized the enormity of trying to explain everything than the time not being right. Similarly, Jesus might have been saying, 'Don't tell anyone until you have the *whole picture*', which will not be the case until the resurrection takes place. Jesus did not want them to mess up. Of Peter, Williams adds that he is the same kind of person as each of us: 'Brought to nothing by his inability to hear and receive the transfiguring presence of God in the helpless and condemned Jesus but called afresh out of his own chaos to the task of finding words for mystery.'

This quote by the former archbishop is revelatory. Amid our own suffering, of course we find it hard to discern transfiguration in a Jesus who is about to be nailed to a cross. In the chaos of our own times, we have a few days to find words to express the mystery of the risen Lord on Easter Day.

So, Jesus' command that the disciples should not say a word about the Transfiguration is one example of a bigger gospel secret to be kept until after the resurrection. The mood certainly changes as soon as Easter arrives. We should be prepared to speak out about the good news when the time is right.

Today's Thought: Do you get the picture yet? Would you feel ready to explain what the Transfiguration means to you? Or would you still rather build a tent?

44

Thursday: Eucharist

At Table Together

Not everything about the pandemic was bad. A bit like those often-told stories about what happened during the war, people will recount their experiences for a generation. Never was so much banana bread made. It is also true that families sat down more often to eat meals together again and enjoyed being at table. John Torode, the Australian-born judge on the UK version of the television cookery competition *MasterChef*, said that he could never understand how people could possibly eat in front of the television anyway. The table is what makes the meal.

Maundy Thursday is significant in the Christian year for a variety of reasons. Christians chiefly remember Jesus' teaching about serving others through his washing of the disciples' feet. This sense of a serving Son of Man is further underlined by his transfiguration of a Jewish Passover meal, in which the bread and wine are proclaimed as Jesus' body and blood. Those who witnessed the spectacle of the institution of the Eucharist did not fully appreciate what he was doing at the time. After the resurrection he is revealed to them in the breaking of the bread.

Each year, classes of school children need to fulfil a curriculum requirement to learn about the practices of the Christian Church. Recently, a group of early teenagers, representing different faiths and none, gathered with me around the altar at St John's Digswell to learn about the Eucharist. I explained the significance of the parish's silver chalices dating back to the eighteenth century and the simple, but lovely, silver plate on which the bread is usually placed. The children adored the candles (of course they wanted to light one) and the colours and the altar book and bells. And they asked a lot of perceptive questions about how and why Christians still connect deeply with the meal Jesus gave the Church on this holy day. 'He just gathered a few friends together for dinner and gave them a real surprise, didn't he?', said one of the boys rather perceptively.

St Paul explains the link between the Eucharist and the suffering and death of Jesus in his first letter to the Corinthians, which sums up the events of this week. In chapter 11 verses 23–26 he recites, almost verbatim, the words of Jesus concerning the bread/his body and the wine/his blood. Foreshadowing the light of Easter to be revealed in a matter of days, Paul continues, 'For whenever you eat this bread and drink this cup, you proclaim the Lord's death until he comes.'

It is always a joy and a privilege to share with others around the table. It is great that, post-pandemic, we have rediscovered this joy. Similarly, after months when it was not permitted to share the elements of Holy Communion – the host and common cup – Christians also rejoiced to be back at table together. It underlined how much many had missed it. A heavenly banquet, a transfigured Passover, in which the lamb is Jesus, through whose death and sacrifice we are baptized into new life, bathed in Transfiguration glory. An invitation like no other.

Today's Thought: What do you like most about being at table with family or friends, and what memories do you have of great celebrations?

45

Good Friday: Jesus, Saviour of the World

Save Us and Help Us

Good Friday is momentous. I have always been surprised that some churches do not hold services on what is the most solemn day of the year. There is no Christian faith or Church without acknowledging the events of today. There are some regular churchgoers who do not attend today. And yet this is the day Jesus died for us! On the other hand, there are people who rarely come to church but always make it on Good Friday. How can we celebrate the resurrection without retracing the steps of the Via Dolorosa – the path of suffering – along which Jesus first carried and was then nailed to his cross as Saviour of the world? I find this perplexing. Perhaps I am overstating it, but I do feel strongly that this is the day of all days.

Of all the titles attributed to or associated with Jesus, some of which we have already considered, 'Saviour' sums up the enormity of the events of today. The title in Greek and Roman civilizations was often applied to emperors, philosophers and gods. But, from the moment when it was used to sum up the saving work of Jesus as both Son of Man and Son of God, it becomes an umbrella term for Jesus, the Saviour who offers salvation to all.

The theme of Jesus the Saviour is strong throughout Luke's Gospel – much more, for example, than is the case in Mark, Matthew and John. Luke has long been thought of as a doctor by profession and stories of healing dominate his Gospel. When, for instance, Jesus says to the woman who is sick, 'Your faith has saved you' (7.50), he is (not for the first time) directly equating faith with healing and salvation for those who witnessed it. When he goes to the house of Zacchaeus the tax collector, who seems to have his life priorities upside down, he explains (again only in Luke) that 'the Son of Man came to seek and to save the lost'. The Saviour is only doing his glorious work when he offers salvation to everyone, Jew and Gentile alike.

The most famous example, also only in Luke, is the thrust of Simeon's response when he first sees the baby Saviour in the Temple in Jerusalem (Luke 2.29–32). Jesus offers salvation to the Gentiles as well as 'the glory of your people Israel'. He gives us the beautiful words of the Nunc Dimittis. We need not fear death because we are in the presence of Jesus, Saviour of the World.

Of course, because Good Friday is a unique day, it necessitates that we view transfiguration in a particular way. Jesus has experienced the loneliness and desolation of Calvary and is temporarily placed in a stranger's tomb. It was the eve of the Jewish sabbath, and now we wait to see what happens next. As the Collect for the Visitation of the Sick (from the 1662 Book of Common Prayer) explains, wonderfully set to music by John Goss (see today's 'Thought' below), we are now on the verge of total redemption. Our wait is finally about to start but, at the same time, it is almost done. We are invited to say the words of the Collect below.

Today's Thought: O Saviour of the World, who by thy cross and precious blood hast redeemed us. Save us and help us, we humbly beseech thee, O Lord.

46

Holy Saturday: Waiting

Most of Our Days Are Like Holy Saturday

Today, Holy Saturday, is perhaps the strangest day in the Christian year. Because nothing really happens. There is a great stillness. A disconcerting silence. There is expectation in the air. But we must just wait. Alan E. Lewis, in his book *Between Cross and Resurrection*, describes it as no man's land and 'an anonymous counterfeit moment in the Gospel story'.

Only St Matthew has any account of what happens on Holy Saturday. The Pharisees and the chief priests go to Pilate and ask him to give the order for Jesus' tomb to be made secure. He also puts a guard on duty for good measure. Meanwhile, Jesus' mother, the other women and his disciples, no doubt bereft with sorrow and incredulous that it has come to this, can do nothing but hide and wait.

So, today, churches are prepared for tomorrow. After the solemnity of Lent, flowers are arranged, white replaces the sombre purple as the liturgical colour, and Easter gardens are made ready. The waiting continues further until later this evening or first thing tomorrow when it is time to revisit the tomb. We will find out what has happened and wait for the first glimpse of the resurrection light and a hint of the promised glory to come.

Of course, like any good novel that you have read more than once, or a movie that is always worth another viewing, we know how the story will turn out in the morning. But we nevertheless hear it again and again – because when the waiting is over the impact on us varies according to our ever-changing circumstances. Only then might we be able to truly explain what happened on Mount Tabor. We will no longer have to keep quiet.

I once heard a Jesuit priest say, 'Most of our days are spent on Holy Saturday.' We get up, do our chores, fill the day with a variety of tasks and then settle down to sleep again before repeating the cycle. Often, nothing happens of any great note or significance and, when it does, it stands out.

Waiting is as counter-cultural as remembering. We do not really like to do it. Impatience abounds. Bishop Martin Warner, in an Easter sermon, suggested that we are living in an age of impatience in which many are wanting a guarantee on their terms. He observes that, 'Most people have given up the challenge and struggle to believe in an unseen glory which is our destiny and they have settled instead for immediate satisfaction, without God. But the evidence of just how satisfying this proves to be does not look encouraging.' Perhaps rediscovering the joy and challenge of waiting, and how that can transfigure our view of life more generally, can be an Easter challenge in the weeks ahead. The waiting is almost over.

Today's Thought: What are you most waiting for when the resurrection dawns this year?

A Prayer

We adore you, O Christ, and we bless you,
because by your holy cross you have redeemed the world.

Questions

Waiting can be a real challenge in our lives, whether waiting for a bus that is late or for the results of a test of some sort. Have you learnt to manage the art of waiting?

How do we address the rise in levels of loneliness in society?

Is Holy Saturday really like every day? 'Where can we live but days?' (Philip Larkin)

Eastertide –
God's *Yes* to Who Jesus Is

'The Transfiguration of our Lord is God's absolute YES to who Jesus is – the promised Messiah – and it is God's absolute YES to our part in being bearers of that world-changing news.'

(Jo Kelly-Moore, Dean of St Albans)

47

Easter Day: Realization Over Time

There Is No Gospel Without the Resurrection

Christ is risen! He is risen indeed! Alleluia!

Ash Wednesday now seems quite some time ago. Early on this Easter Sunday morning, our journey through Lent comes to what is at first an inauspicious climax. The baffled and buffeted friends of Jesus realize that the tomb is empty and initially they are filled with uncertainty.

So much has happened. So deep has been the sorrow of seeing their friend executed in the most barbaric of ways. So many insights have been gleaned into who Jesus is, without being able to utter a single word to anyone. And now, a deep sense of loneliness and isolation is tinged with resurrection hope. Their bereft state never seems far from the surface. They remain inherently vulnerable. Can he possibly have been true to his word and risen from the dead?

But it is true, the tomb is empty. In fact, as it gradually dawns on those close to Jesus over the next few weeks, the glory previously revealed on the holy mountain is now dramatically augmented through the resurrection. Centuries of sinfulness are transfigured, and years of expectancy are now fulfilled before their eyes. But it will take some time for realization to set in.

For many Christians, today begins with the holy fire. It is a strange custom, rooted in the Orthodox tradition, but one that ignites the hopes of Christians worldwide. A flickering flame of light pierces the darkness of a church building as the radiancy of the resurrection gradually permeates the space. This visual progression of light is a deeply spiritual symbol too.

No doubt mindful of many of the psalms which formed the backdrop to Jewish worship in their day, Psalm 73 would surely have been a source of great encouragement: 'You guide me with your counsel, and afterwards you will take me into glory' (v. 24). The disciples and the first believers of the good news were now presented with a mammoth task. The first Christian evangelists had to tell others the news and, at the same time, convince them.

'For the early Christians, the gospel without the resurrection was no gospel at all,' writes Bishop Michael Ramsey in his book *The Resurrection of Christ*, adding that, in retrospect, 'Calvary is no disaster which needs the resurrection to reverse it, but a victory to signal that the resurrection follows quickly to seal it.' Calvary has been sealed by Jesus' defeat of death once and for all. The resurrection light has triumphed over the world's darkness.

The glory now framed by our Lord's resurrection is our key priority as Jesus' disciples today. We are to be witnesses of the resurrection, without which there is no good news. Remember how the greatly courageous Dietrich Bonhoeffer said that it is grace that is most necessary in rising to the challenge of service. This wonderful prayer used on the feast of St Stephen, the first martyr of the Church, can also be ours as we light our candle and proclaim again: Christ is risen! He is risen indeed! Alleluia. Happy Easter.

A prayer for today

God give you grace to be faithful witnesses to see the heavens opened and the glory of God in the face of Jesus.
Amen.

48

Easter Monday: The Gospel of Glory

The Whole Encounter

Today, we will stay a little with Bishop Ramsey, for when I used to speak with him as my mentor on the Transfiguration in Durham, he was always interested in why John's Gospel, which takes the theme of the glory very seriously, omitted the Transfiguration story altogether:

> The Transfiguration is omitted, for the glory belongs not to any isolated episodes but to the story as a whole ... the tradition of the Transfiguration has left its mark upon the thought and language of the writer. His Gospel is indeed the Gospel of glory.
>
> (Michael Ramsey, *The Glory of God and the Transfiguration of Christ*)

The Fourth Gospel is often divided into two sections: the Book of Signs (John 1—12) and the Book of Glory (John 13—20, or 21 if you include the epilogue). But it can also be argued that the whole story of Jesus in this Gospel is an explanation of the Transfiguration. This glory reflects the unique relationship between God the Father and God the Son, which continually fascinates John and takes up a great deal of his gospel story. Whoever has seen Jesus has seen the Father; the Father and the Son are one; Jesus will be seen for a little while before returning to his true home with the Father. In all of this, the glory plays a key role.

Weeks of celebration and storytelling reflect the Easter season which is now underway. The glory of Jesus shines forth through the events of Calvary and the empty tomb, as we encounter the risen Jesus afresh and again in many ways, for ever mindful of the magnificent scene we witnessed on the summit of Mount Tabor.

St John's teaching is that it is through (the now risen) Jesus that God continues to make himself known in Eastertide: for 'No one has ever seen God, but the one and only Son, who is himself God and is in the closest relationship with the Father, has made him known' (1.18). This should be a verse we write out and keep in our wallet or purse, next to our phone or on our screensaver.

The Father and the Son together have presented us with a vision of transformative light and love. They have dealt with the suffering of the world and overcome the darkness that often invades our lives. The whiteness of Jesus' face on the holy mountain reflected God's glory, seen in the Son, so that the light of the world could be made known. And the promise of the Holy Spirit to ensure that we will not be left alone is real.

In this glorious Eastertide, we thank God for a renewed encounter with the God of glory. We praise him through his Son, our Saviour, who has given us the good news of salvation.

A prayer for today

The Lord is exalted over all the nations,
　　his glory above the heavens.
Who is like the Lord our God,
　　the one who sits enthroned on high?

(Psalm 113.4–5)

49

Eastertide: A Veiled Gospel

Overcoming Blindness

If St John's is the Gospel that summarizes our encounter with the God of glory, it is to St Paul's extensive letters to the early Church that we can look for more explanations and insights into the working out of this mystery.

To live the Christian life is to wrestle daily with how we pass on the good news to others. It often involves overcoming huge hurdles. At the start of our pilgrimage, I mentioned St Columba, who left Ireland to bring the good news to the British. I am sure he also encountered many cultural, linguistic and practical barriers to proclaiming the resurrection in a foreign land. It is part of the work of any evangelist to recognize the context in which they are placed.

Many of these challenges are principally down to human folly or a basic lack of understanding as to what our priorities are as Jesus' disciples. We are so easily distracted, as any parish priest will tell you! In his many letters to the emerging Church, Paul returns, again and again, to this central theme – understand the context, get your priorities right, don't hold back in ministry, why complicate matters?

Perhaps the most important verse in St Paul in this regard is:

And even if our gospel is veiled, it is veiled to those who are perishing. The god of this age has blinded the minds of unbelievers, so that they cannot see the light of the gospel that displays the glory of Christ, who is the image of God. (2 Corinthians 4.3–4)

Paul is here being characteristically honest and to the point. In other places, the apostle writes of Jesus as the new Moses and of the resurrection inaugurating a new covenant. He desires simply that the faithful focus fully on Jesus. But questioning, cynicism and unbelief are just some of the reasons people remain blind to the glory of Jesus, resulting in what might colloquially be called divine-light deprivation. Paul takes all of this into account.

Immediately after each of the three Gospel stories of the Transfiguration, the account of the inability of Jesus' disciples to cast demons out of a young boy is the first main event to be reported (see Mark 9.14–29). It is fascinating that in Raphael's majestic painting of the Transfiguration (to be enjoyed in the Vatican and, if unable to visit it in person, online), the depiction of the story of the young boy, his family and the disciples is prominent in the foreground while the Transfiguration is vividly portrayed behind. The two stories are interrelated and help explain each other. This is done chiefly by showing everyone in the painting to be pointing to the transfigured Jesus. Nothing can be achieved or done without him. That is the point of today. It all revolves now around Jesus in Eastertide and now we can talk openly and freely of his work. Raphael paints the glory of God radiant through Jesus as Messiah. He is vindicated by Moses and Elijah basking in Transfiguration whiteness – a reminder to those involved in the young boy's spiritual welfare that their eyes still need to be opened. The veil must be lifted, so that the good news can be seen in all its glory.

The hidden theme of this painting is faith. By opening our eyes to the radiancy of the resurrection glory we pray too that our eyes may be constantly opened to the reality of the glory of the Father as revealed in the risen Lord. Then, like the first witnesses, we may share the good news with others.

A prayer for today

In your resurrection, O Jesus,
let heaven and earth rejoice, Alleluia!

50

Wait, There's More!
The Story Is Far From Over

The Life of the World to Come

In the celebrated Easter story of the road to Emmaus, two of Jesus' followers fail to recognize who he is (Luke 24.13–35). They walk and talk with Jesus, but their eyes are kept from recognizing him. Only after persuading him to stay for a meal, as it was getting late, did they recognize him as he broke the bread. As the veil is lifted from their eyes he disappears from their sight.

There are several resurrection stories in the final chapters of the four Gospels. Each is different. They suggest random and unexpected appearances. Doubt, faith and drama abound. Most of all, however, those to whom Jesus appears are increasingly assured that his promise of the transfiguration of suffering and death and the bringing of new life for all is happening before their eyes. The glory of the resurrection, glimpsed on the Transfiguration mountain, changes their faith and expectation for ever. In a few weeks' time, Jesus will ascend and be reunited with his Father in heaven (Luke 24.51).

The Nicene Creed fails to mention the Transfiguration. But, interestingly, it does affirm a belief 'in the resurrection of the dead and the life of the world to come'. This stark and confident statement of faith emphasizes that we are not quite there yet and that there is more to come. 'The world to come' suggests a time and place in salvation history when the final things, talked about often at many levels, will come to pass when God's glory will be perfected, fully restored, once and for all.

Christians believe that Jesus was conceived, born, baptized, ministered for a relatively short time, was transfigured, betrayed, suffered, died, rose again from the dead and ascended into the heaven. The connection between life so far and a Second Coming has fascinated experts since the first century and continues to do so today. We do not know when a Second Coming will happen. Or how. We cannot be sure what the signs will be. A casual glance at the state of the world today, and the state of God's creation which was gifted to humankind, often leads people to an expression of contemporary lamentation and causes genuine worry and concern. Very often this then leads on to thoughts about final judgement and future glory. It might not be in vogue to talk about such matters from a theological point of view, but it is a concern for a lot of people. Particularly of course around the associated issues of climate change and what we have done to the planet. Where is our world heading?

Writing in the last century, G. H. Boobyer in *St Mark and the Transfiguration Story* suggested that far from being the end of the story, what we see on the Transfiguration mountain is not yet the fullest vision: 'There is a vision yet to come when the Son has been glorified with the glory that he had with the Father before the world began, and the disciples are led to the vision of this glory (John 17.5 and 24; 1 John 3.2).' This leaves some to suggest that the Transfiguration is a kind of cinema trailer for an event that will come at a yet unknown time – when the glimpsed glory will be established more fully and for ever. Namely, when Jesus returns as he promised to do.

The 2 Peter account of the Transfiguration, which is important for many reasons, is framed in terms of a future coming of which this, the Transfiguration, is but a foretaste. In the opening verse of this account (printed at the start of this book) you will see that the apostle talks about 'the coming of Our Lord Jesus Christ in power' and the fact that they were 'eye-witnesses of his majesty'. This is written after the Transfiguration, passion, resurrection and ascension have taken place. The whole thrust of this apostolic hope is that Jesus will come again, and his glory will be finally and ultimately revealed.

That waiting will go on. We live for now joyously in the fact that death has been defeated through the risen and glorious Lord. Our task is to continue to be bearers of the good news of the resurrection and of God's glory in which we share fully wherever we are today. Dean Jo Kelly-Moore told me shortly after I met her as an Honorary Canon of St Albans Abbey, where she now serves, 'The Transfiguration of our Lord is God's absolute YES to who Jesus is – the promised Messiah – and it is God's absolute YES to our part in being bearers of that world-changing news.'

As our Lenten pilgrimage comes to an end, we know it is just a beginning. We need to stay with our transfigured Jesus every day of our lives. Try not to forget how important it is. Keep the events of what happened there close to you.

One simple way of doing this is to take a frequent look online or in person at the Transfiguration stained-glass window in Durham Cathedral, which is also the cover of this book. Designed by Tom Denny, this remarkable piece of work, created in memory of Bishop Ramsey, encapsulates our individual involvement in the consequences of what happened on the mountain. The local hero St Cuthbert, a disciple of Columba whose final resting place in the same cathedral is close to the window, looks on within the window. Cuthbert, one of the most celebrated of the Celtic saints, represents you and me – pondering what saying YES to our risen and glorious Jesus means for you and all of us in the Church today.

In a world where nothing can really be taken for granted, I hope that our journey to the mountain with its plentiful motifs has been both a challenging and stimulating one. Now, free from our Lord's command to say nothing until the time is right, we can finally seize the moment and recognize the importance of communicating this glorious gospel of the Transfiguration fully aware of an increasingly challenging context.

A prayer for today

Lord of all life and power,
who through the mighty resurrection of your Son
overcame the old order of sin and death
to make all things new in him:
grant that we, being dead to sin
and alive to you in Jesus Christ,
may reign with him in glory;
to whom with you and the Holy Spirit
be praise and honour, glory and might,
now and in all eternity.
Amen.

(Collect for Easter Day, Common Worship*)*

References

John Barton, *A History of the Bible: The Book and Its Faiths*, London: Penguin, 2020.

Pope Benedict XVI, *Jesus of Nazareth*, London: Bloomsbury, 2007.

Dietrich Bonhoeffer, *The Cost of Discipleship*, new edn, London: SCM Press, 2015.

Dietrich Bonhoeffer, *Letters and Papers from Prison*, SCM Classics, London: SCM Press, 2001.

G. H. Boobyer, *St Mark and the Transfiguration Story*, Edinburgh: T & T Clark, 1942.

Jean de la Bruyère, *Les Caractères*, Paris, 1688.

John Bunyan, *Pilgrim's Progress*, Fearn: Christian Focus Publications, 2005.

John Paul Heil, *The Transfiguration of Jesus*, Rome: Pontificio Istituto Biblico, 2000.

Dorothy Lee, *Transfiguration*, London: Continuum, 2004.

Christy Lefteri, *The Beekeeper of Aleppo*, London: Manilla Press, 2020.

Alan E. Lewis, *Between Cross and Resurrection: A Theology of Holy Saturday*, Grand Rapids, MI: Eerdmans, 2003.

J. Philip Newell, *Celtic Benediction: Morning and Night Prayer*, Norwich: Canterbury Press, 2000.

Henri Nouwen, *Reaaching Out*, London: Collins, 1976.

Boniface Ramsey, *Beginning to Read the Fathers*, rev. edn, Mahwah, NJ: Paulist Press, 2012.

Michael Ramsey, *The Resurrection of Christ: An Essay in Biblical Theology*, London: Geoffrey Bles, 1950.

Michael Ramsey, *The Glory of God and the Transfiguration of Jesus*, London: Longmans, Green & Co., 1949.

Kenneth Stevenson, *Rooted in Detachment, Living the Transfiguration*, London: Darton, Longman & Todd, 2007.

Tom Whipple, 'Why is the world getting sadder?', *The Times*, 27 March 2023.

Rowan Williams, *Meeting God in Mark: Reflections for the Season of Lent*, London: SPCK, 2014.